MIKE FOLEY

BUSY AS HELL

STORIES, LEGENDS, TALL TALES, YARNS AND A CAST OF CHARACTERS FROM THE BOSTON FIRE DEPARTMENT'S FAMED WAR YEARS.

To John,

One of my oldest and best friends.

All the best

Mike

This book is a memoir. The author has attempted to recreate events, locales and conversations from his memories of them. The opinions expressed within this book are solely his own and as he remembered them. The author does not assume and hereby disclaims any liability to any party for any loss, damage, or disruption caused by errors or omissions, whether such errors or omissions result from negligence, accident, or any other cause.

Copyright © 2015 by MIKE FOLEY
All rights reserved.

First Edition: December 2015

Cover Design and Layout: K.R. Conway
Editor: Marie DeRoma
Photos: Unless otherwise noted, all photos are courtesy of the legendary Bill Noonan, BFD

Copyright © 2015 by Mike Foley. All rights reserved. In accordance with U.S. Copyright Act of 1976, the scanning, uploading and electronic sharing of any part of this book without the permission of the publisher / author is unlawful piracy and theft of the author's intellectual property. If you would like to use material from this book (other than for review purposes), prior written permission must be obtained by contacting the publisher at mike@BFDbusyashell.com. Thank you for your support of the author's rights.

Library of Congress Cataloging-in-Publication Data
Foley, Mike
Busy As Hell/ by Mike Foley – First Edition.
   Pages: 323
   Summary: A veteran fire fighter reflects on the stories and tales told by his brothers and superiors during the famed War Years of the Boston Fire Department, from 1963 to 1983.

M. Foley
P.O. Box 1921
Sandwich, MA 02563

ISBN: 978-1522755333

Published in the United States of America

"Ladder 4 returning"
L to R: Jim Sheedy, John Gaddis, Jim Coakley. (FF Sheedy was killed in the line of duty on October 1, 1964.)

Photo by Joe Farren

DEDICATION

This book is lovingly dedicated to my grandfather, father, and brother - three men who faithfully served and protected the people of the city of Boston for 46, 42, and 30 years, respectively:

District Fire Chief Michael G. Foley, District 6
(1917-1963)

Fire Lieutenant Robert P. Foley, Ladder 7
(1945-1987)

Fire Fighter John P. Foley, Engine 21
(1974-2004)

PROLOGUE

Permit me to awaken an agile snippet of Shakespearean brilliance so that I may offer you a singular glimpse inside the character of the men you will meet on the ensuing pages. Those of us who have served know there is much to be said for the similarities inherent in our brotherhoods, ours forged on Boston's red fire engines and Billy Shakespeare's forged in England by fifteenth century warriors:

We few, we happy few, we band of brothers;
For he to-day that sheds his blood with me
Shall be my brother; be he ne'er so vile,
This day shall gentle his condition;
And gentlemen in England now-a-bed
Shall think themselves accurs'd they were not here,
And hold their manhoods cheap whiles any speaks
That fought with us upon Saint Crispin's day.

That's us. The band of brothers who fought, not at the Battle of Agincourt, but up the stairs and down the stairs, in buildings tall and not so tall, along hallways long and short, through windows big and small, on roof tops flat and pitched, in attics under the roof, in cellars under the floor, beside the water, in and out of the water, in cellars below cellars, in front of walls and behind walls, at daybreak and dusk, at high noon and in the middle of the night, aboard ships and boats, over fences and other dividers, inside and outside, feet on the ground and on rungs of ladders, in hot weather and cold and weather in between, under clear skies and cloudy skies, during droughts and ice storms and rainstorms and hurricanes and blizzards. But together, always together.

INTRODUCTION

Sprinkled throughout the following pages, while, yes, you will find some of my own, first-person recollections, make no mistake, this isn't even close to being an autobiography. The standard has already been set for such ventures - New York City's Dennis Smith stepped up and led the fire fighter's charge in 1972 with his all-time and international classic, *Report From Engine Company 82*. Then, in 1983, Boston Deputy Fire Chief, Leo Stapleton, did us proud with *Thirty Years On The Line*.

Instead, what you now hold in your hands is a hitherto unwritten history, one that reaches out to the now titled "cast of characters" and draws on their remembrances of the kinds of incidents that never made the newspapers, a part and parcel to the private lore of the nation's oldest fire department. Think of it as the inside edition of an oral tradition. These are the yarns you'd hear and laugh about if you were gathered around the kitchen table in any Boston fire house. These are the stories snatched from the true (but unofficial) annals of the Boston Fire Department, circa 1963 through 1983, and passed along for the generations of firefighters to come. But what to write about? What to include, what to leave out? Let me tell you that after having spoken to scores of fire fighters about this project, and out of the hundreds and hundreds of tales they told and I heard, it was no easy task deciding which stories would make the cut and which would not. Short of writing *Busy As Hell II* - actually, a thought - in the interests of accuracy mixed with caution (and with just a pinch of a sense of right and wrong) I adhered to the following general guidelines:

What is included are: (1) stories and tall tales told by firemen about themselves and the incidents in which they participated, (2) stories and anecdotes that were witnessed or recounted by a sufficient number of people to render them factual and which hurt no one (3) stories about men who have gone to their eternal reward but who probably wouldn't mind us talking about them today and, finally (4) stories that some people may not want revealed but, because the stories are widely known about and accepted, or too good to leave out, I went ahead and told them without mentioning any names, tricky guy that I am.

What was left out was any obscure or little-known story that could even remotely be considered as telling stories out of school, or talking poorly about, or unduly besmirching the memory of those who are no longer here to defend themselves. In other words, there aren't any *Enquirer*-like revelations here.

Now I understand and accept that to those who weren't there, some of the stories, tall tales, legends, and yarns may seem to betray a confidence. I thought about that and decided that when all was said and done, if the stories, even the bad ones, were already widely known, well, I just went ahead and included them, secure in the feeling that I wasn't blowing the whistle on anyone.

So, for the stories that did make the cut, they stand on their own. There has been no attempt to evade, slant, or sugarcoat anything. In a phrase, this isn't all fun and games. Yeah, there's a ton of funny stuff on the ensuing pages but there's some pretty serious stuff in here, too - like, for one, what it was like to work with a fireman who set buildings on fire in his spare, off-duty time and then, too, while he was working.

I can state with confidence that *Busy As Hell* is often funny, often serious, often instructive and, yes, an often critical look at the good and bad experiences shared by hundreds of men who forged a path for themselves through the busiest years ever experienced by Boston's happy band of swashbuckling firemen. And while we're on the subject of these men, and yes, just men, all of their stories, tall tales, and legends were lived, established and recounted before there was a female fire fighter in Boston (in

1984). Sorry gals.

So then, what was it like being a member of the Boston Fire Department back then? And too...what about the fires? Well, the facts and statistics and records are verifiable and therefore undeniable - the records confirm that the twenty-one years between 1963 and 1983 was the busiest time in the BFD's history. This period became known as "The War Years," affectionately by those who served during this time and with no small measure of awe and envy by those who came along after.

While perusing the records and trying to add some perspective to the truths they presented, it occurred to me that contemporary Boston firemen may find it difficult to believe that we old guys were really as busy as we claim to have been. The temptation exists, I'm sure, to pigeonhole us with the old people who walked uphill both ways to school during a blizzard and without a coat because, well, that's what old guys do, isn't it? Wax poetic with words like, "Now, when I was a kid blah, blah, blah . . . "

But reality is there for all to see. New guys, those with ten or less years of service, may not have seen as many fires in their fledgling careers that we might have seen in two or three months. No, I'm serious. It was that busy back then.

Now when I say fires, I'm talking about times when

you actually had to run a line of hose and squirt some water inside a building on fire - and not just at a pile of rubbish or junk - or where you pull enough ceilings to make your arms wish they'd never become part of your body. I'm talking about real fires.

To illustrate the point, I worked a night tour of duty in the early 1970s with the crew of Ladder 23. During the sixteen hours from 4:00 PM until we were relieved at 8:00 AM the following day, we went to ten fires, the kind of fires that required at least three engine companies and two ladder companies to extinguish. There was one of what we then called a "working fire," three multiple alarm fires and six one or two room fires. When you mix in the requisite number of false alarms and car fires, etc., well, we didn't spend more than 90 minutes in the fire house all night. Now I certainly didn't work this tour alone. There were probably fifty firemen from different companies who also went to those fires. When the tour was finally over, I remember accepting the adage that the toughest job on the fire department was "a rake man on a busy truck."

Research tells us that during the years 1963-1983, there were close to 6000 working fires and multiple alarm fires in the city of Boston. That is, fires that required more than the three first alarm engines and two first alarm ladder companies to extinguish.

Also during this same time period - and this is an evaluation made by a group of former firemen I polled, trusted members all - it is estimated there were probably at least the same number of fires that did not require any additional help to extinguish. These are the so-called "one-alarm" fires which, in many circles, are considered some of the worst kinds of fires to fight, a fact that demands some explanation.

During the early part of the war years, there were still a fair number of so-called "One Building, One Alarm" fire chiefs working. These were the chiefs who for reasons known only to themselves, decided that a burning building, any burning building at all, deserved only the basic response of firemen to extinguish the fire. We all surmised that there were a couple of reasons for this: (1) some district chiefs didn't like certain deputy chiefs and wouldn't call for more help because if they did, the deputy would show up and assume command, (2) some chiefs just didn't believe the extra help was ever necessary; they never needed any more help than the bare minimum. They knew they had good firemen working for them . . . firemen who brought plenty of hose, plenty of water and plenty of tools and ladders with them to the battle, and collectively, men with no shortage of tenacity and grit, firemen determined to put the fire out and go home. Of course, we also believed that some of them took perverse pleasure in working our asses off.

There was a hidden element to the equation, one that presented itself because some of the old-time chiefs hated paperwork. The last thing they wanted to do was go to a fire, stand around for an hour or two while the troops went about their business and then go back to the fire house and fill out fire reports. So they did the next best thing - they decided that a burned out three-story building was nothing more than a pile of rubbish and called it such. This saved them a ton of paperwork because all they had to do to report a rubbish fire was to call it, well, a rubbish fire. The adverse effect was that legitimate fires were lost to history, never to be counted and, so, added to the annual totals. I doubt this practice ever had a direct effect on company closings and the like but it damn sure didn't help when the bean counters started snooping around, looking for places to cut the department's budget.

These men weren't dangerous, per se, just tough as nails. These were the old depression-era and WWII guys, firemen appointed in the 1920s, 30s and 40s; men who worked for decades without anything even approaching modern day equipment like, for instance, gloves. Once, when I had about fifteen minutes on the job, an old-time district chief - I still don't know who he was - told me that wearing gloves made me look stupid. Us old timers didn't need no stinkin' gloves, he was probably thinking, why should this young whipper snapper wear them?

So, I did the only thing I could do . . . I took them off. Can't be lookin' stupid in front of the chief, you know.

One of the BFD's enduring legends - the story is outside the war years focus of this book but bears telling - will set the capstone on the picture for you. It's the saga of a certain district chief in South Boston who didn't want anyone but South Boston firemen at his fires unless it was absolutely necessary. He rarely wore his helmet and fire coat, preferring his crumpled old uniform cap and uniform sack coat. He was the quintessential tough-as-nails, old-time bad-ass. A chief who once took care of a touchy situation in the fire house with a one-punch knock out of a Lieutenant who'd called him an "Irish son-of-a-bitch." There were some things you just didn't say to Irish tough guys. This chief had a pretty cool nickname, too: "Iron Mike."

Old-time firemen I met over the years used to say he was once seen standing in front of a burning building on West Broadway in South Boston watching as (third due) Engine 7 and (second due) Ladder 17 approached the fire from over the bridge and their quarters in the nearby South End - which is never to be confused with South Boston - only to see the chief waving them past the fire, in essence, telling them to keep the hell going, get the hell out of South Boston and get the hell back to the South End. This legend has a special place in my heart because the chief in question was my grandfather, Michael G. Foley, late of District 6. Of course, I wasn't there to see any of this but as the years went by and the legend grew, there were at least 2875 firemen riding on those two fire engines that day, that is to say, way more than enough to take delight in repeating the story.

Getting back to the war years - owing to a One-Building, One-Alarm chief's ideas about how to command, the first alarm fire companies would often be tied up at fires for more than long enough to satisfy these interesting idiosyncrasies. Conventional wisdom among the rank and file firemen was often quite different: Get all the guys we need to put the damned fire out so we can go home.

But in the final analysis, idiosyncrasies trumped the rank and file and while we may not have been better off for it, it sure added some swagger to our legacy for while we might have bitched and complained about the lack of help, we also took no small measure of pride in having been there. I like to think of it as The St. Crispin's Day effect.

These kinds of bosses, and there were several, also

displayed a singular distrust in letting anyone know what was going on at the fires at which they were in charge; the *I've Got A Secret* chiefs we called them. This command approach was characterized by their obvious lack of willingness to relay any information to the Fire Alarm Office (or tuned-in fire buffs and sparks), even when prodded. As an example, here's a memorable composite (but wholly typical) of a 2:00 AM radio transmission from one of the more stingy chiefs, one in District 5:

Fire Alarm Office: "Box 2265 struck for a fire on Marcella Street near Highland. Okay Car 5?"

No answer from Car 5.

60 seconds later: "Engine 42 has fire showing on Marcella Street."

Fire Alarm replies: "Okay Engine 42, you have fire showing on Marcella Street."

Two milliseconds later: "Car 5 is off on Marcella Street."

Fire Alarm acknowledges: "Okay, Car 5, you're off on Marcella Street."

Translation….60 seconds ago, the chief didn't answer the radio because he wasn't in his car yet. (This is long before portable radios were issued.) Yet, the instant Engine 42 reported fire showing, the chief (or most likely, his driver) reported that he was off on Marcella Street, allegedly meaning he was actually there, when he almost assuredly wasn't even out of the fire house yet. But by calling off on Marcella Street, he stopped all radio traffic from the fire ground. It meant that he was actually there and in charge. Even if he wasn't. This also means that by being off the air, he had no plans to communicate any time soon.

Then, some thirty to forty minutes later, you may hear:

"Fire Alarm calling Car 5. Can we have a report on box 2265?"

To which the chief might reply - and this was actually heard more than once: "Car 5 reports that fire fighting operations are continuing at box 2265."

The not-so-hidden meaning was that the companies at the fire on Marcella Street - Engines 42, 14, 24 and Ladders 30 (RIP) and 4 - were up to their collective eyeballs in hose, water, ladders, and tools but the chief didn't want anyone else showing up to help.

Like any walk of life, our bosses had different personalities. It was the officer's job to evaluate them accurately and then figure out the best way to get along. It all worked out in the end because we survived and while we did, it was easy to conclude that while some chiefs were better than others, they were all good, capable men.

The very same could be said for the Lieutenants

and Captains. They're the men who sit in the front seat of the front-line fire companies and run the small shows that, when combined, make up the big shows. When they arrive at a fire - and 90% of the time, it's before the district chief arrives - it is their job to assess the nature and extent of the fire and to, if necessary, request more help. Generally speaking, officers come in three categories: (1) exceptional; there were scores, (2) great; there were many and (3) not so great; there were a few, sprinkled here and there.

What makes a good officer? Well, first and foremost, they must be technically proficient; they have to know what the hell they're doing. When they climb down from the front seat of a fire engine and start giving orders, they better not make any mistakes. At least not any serious ones.

A company officer must balance initiative and enthusiasm with sound judgment. It is no small matter to decide when it is proper to lead men inside a building on fire or when to stay outside.

A good fire officer must be dependable and predictable . . . predictable in the sense that the fire fighters have to know their boss will always be even mannered and won't fall to pieces at the first sign of chaos.

Any fire department functions within a para-military system. Just like any of our military services, the rank structure is there for a reason. It sets up a basic system of authority that is understood by everyone. The system also demands the same kind of obedience to orders because, again, just like our military services, the situations to which the fire department responds demands quick, efficient and accurate action on the part of those in attendance. There isn't any room for discussion about what to do and when to do it. Decisions aren't referred to a committee for discussion. Fighting a fire has the same basic ingredients as fighting a military battle - it's Us vs. The Enemy. So when one of the bosses says, "Get a line started to the front door," no one believes this is the time for analysis or oversight. The boss said run the line – you run the line. Period.

The years between 1963 and 1983 found the BFD heavily populated with military veterans, all of whom were broken down into three separate groups: the WWII guys, the Korean War guys, and the Vietnam guys. This was a fortunate situation for the people of Boston because the department greatly benefited from the experience these men had garnered during three wars. It meant that almost everyone was experienced in taking orders - always a good thing - and many had experience giving orders, another good thing. It also meant that almost to a man, there wasn't much worse for their eyes to see after having slugged it out with the

Japanese in the Pacific and East Asia, the Germans in Europe, the North Koreans and Chinese in Korea, or the NVA and Viet Cong in Southeast Asian mountains and jungles.

Okay, back to the stats: When one-alarm fires are added to the working fires and multiples and when the fires lost to history are estimated, it means that between 1963 and 1983, there were about 13,500 serious fires in Boston.

That's 643 per year or one every 13.6 hours.

For 21 years.

In a city of about 600,000 inhabitants. A city less than one-quarter the population of Brooklyn, New York.

Busy as hell, indeed.

A further appraisal of the facts and records will also verify that about two-thirds of these 13,500 fires occurred in a section of Boston the fire department refers to as Division 2, the area roughly west and south of Massachusetts Avenue, an arbitrary dividing line placed on a city map to differentiate between Divisions 1 and 2, largely for administrative purposes.

Division 2 consists mostly of the small towns that were consolidated and/or annexed to Boston beginning in the latter years of the nineteenth century. It contains about 65% of Boston's land area and its streets are lined with large numbers or closely situated wooden homes. It is home to the large portion of Boston's static population and includes neighborhoods called Fenway/Kenmore, Jamaica Plain, Roxbury, Dorchester, Roslindale, Mattapan, Hyde Park and West Roxbury

Division 1 consists of the area roughly east and north of the same Massachusetts Avenue. Structurally, it is far more diverse than Division 2 for here you'll find the high-rise office buildings in the downtown and financial districts and the tourist-type sites that Boston is most famous for: Beacon Hill and its tiny, cobblestone streets filled with three and four story tenements, the Freedom Trail, Faneuil Hall, the Boston Common and Public Gardens and the State House. Like any downtown area, it is home to a significant day-time, transient work force transient population. I don't have any specific numbers to cite but I'd guess that there are regularly as many as 100-200,000 people working in Boston proper during the day, people who don't live in downtown Boston and who go home to other cities and towns after work. Division 1 also includes the areas of South and East Boston and Charlestown, all of which are structurally more like the neighborhoods in Division 2, and the so-called "South End," a smallish area jammed with brownstone-type dwellings, which once upon a time housed a then-poorer populace.

The South End was the scene of many of Boston's fires beginning in the mid-1950s and on to the mid-1960s. The area is an amazing story unto itself because it withstood the stigma of decay and destruction to stand as testament to the results of intelligent urban planning and gentrification. At one time, you could buy an old, run-down four story brick building by paying the back taxes, most of those same buildings are worth upwards of a million dollars, or more. However, and while including these three sections of the city, the static, overnight population in Division 1 is much less than in Division 2.

We may safely conclude that the reason for the disparity in the number of fires during this time period is obvious; there are tens of thousands more people living in Division 2 than there are in Division 1. This fact should also verify a long-held belief of mine . . . the three main causes of fires in any building you've ever been in are men, women, and children.

There was an often and not-so-subtle competition between the two divisions, some just for fun, some not so much. The scales were tipped depending on your viewpoint . . . which division you worked in. The competition was pointed and healthy because it sharpened everyone's skills and helped immeasurably whenever firemen from both divisions teamed up to defeat a common enemy. The fun part, the chest-beating and such, usually took place at social gatherings and included bragging rights and other testosterone driven analysis:

"You Division 2 firemen are a bunch of pretenders - going to fake fires in little wooden houses. Any building that you can walk through in less than a minute isn't a building at all!"

"Ha! You Division 1 guys get a two-cent fire in one room of a giant building, strike a bunch of extra alarms and Division 2 guys have to go all the way downtown to put it out for you."

Or, my very favorite, delivered by a Division 2 guy, the coup de grâce, "If you've spent your whole career in Division 1, you can *remember* all the fires you went to."

For myself, I've always thought of the differences as being not unlike those of WWII. Division 1 was like the European Theater of Operations (ETO), a larger production involving larger buildings and with more logistics involved. Division 2 was more like the war in the Pacific; a series of well-attended barroom brawls. Attack a little island (the fire), get your ass kicked a bit, prevail and then go on to the next battle.

When you sprinkle in the personalities and experiences of the district and division commanders, it made matters more interesting. For instance, there were times when certain bosses didn't want help from anyone in the other division. I'm sure the attitudes were founded a hundred years ago when most of the fires were in the downtown and mercantile and waterfront areas. The men who worked in those companies back then were the heavy hitters. Those who worked in the residential areas were the pretenders; they were the guys with trees and shrubs and things lining their streets. Of course, as time went on, the fire load increased and shifted. The outlying companies started doing more and more work. The downtown companies, while their work load remained about the same for a while, were eventually overtaken. In later years, the work load was such that two-thirds of all the fires in Boston were in Division 2.

Okay, three more points before we get rolling . . . throughout the book, I will use the terms "firefighter," "fireman," and "Jake" interchangeably. Yes, I am well aware of the union position that states that "firefighters fight fires, firemen stoke boilers." But in reality it's just a technical (though real) differentiation the union adopted decades ago with the belief that doing so would add a level of professionalism to an otherwise non-professional sounding designation. That being said, the reader should draw no conclusion or inference about my use of the other, so-called non-union term "fireman" for it is only what it is . . . a random word on a random page, nothing more.

You will not see the word "hero" anywhere in this book, except in this tiny paragraph.

Why? Because I refuse to use it. In my opinion, it's a fairly recent media creation used to describe every member of the military and every manner of public servant. Everyone's a hero these days, even politicians. Everything everyone does is heroic. Yet, in all my life, I have never, ever heard a fireman call himself a hero or describe anything he did as heroic. And I've never heard one fireman call another fireman a hero. It's ridiculous. So there.

Alas, and this may be a concern for some of you, there is the issue of salty language. We all know the words; we've all used them from time to time, some more than others. My benchmark was to keep them in the story when their usage was necessary to the story's impact. You will see them every now and then and I believe you will agree with me that sometimes there just isn't any substitute for a good, old-fashioned cuss word.

So now that we have all of qualifiers out of the way, let me suggest that if you listen closely you'll hear the old fashioned house gong go off, hear the man on patrol announce the location, feel yourself slide the brass pole to the main floor, grab the strap on the back step of that pump, or if you're a truckie, curl your arm around the railing on the side of that old, rickety spare ladder truck, as off we go!

GLOSSARY OF TERMS

Apparatus - The fire engines themselves. Can be an engine company, a ladder company, a rescue, or a tower ladder. Also called "the piece," as in "Park the piece over there," or, "apparatus" as in "Is the apparatus clear for a response?" NOTES: (1) Boston fire engines are **never** referred to as "fire trucks." Never! (2) Boston fire engines are not called "rigs." That's a decidedly New York term.

Big Line - a length of fire hose, usually 200 to 250-feet long, consisting of 50-foot lengths of hose, 2½ inches in diameter, and coupled together. This is the hose most commonly used for (1) an interior attack when large quantities of water are needed, (2) an attack from outside when large quantities of water are needed or (3) when supplying heavy stream appliances.

Company Officer - A fire officer, typically a lieutenant or captain, who leads a team of three or more firefighters in a front line fire company.

Division - Approximately one-half the city of Boston. Commanded by a Deputy Fire Chief.

District - sub units within a Division, Commanded by a District Fire Chief. There are nine fire districts in Boston.

Engine company - The fire engine that carries the hose. Generally, these are the guys who squirt the water on the fires. The fire engine itself, the pump, is used to supply all the water needed from the beginning to the end of any and all fires. Without an engine company, fires would never go out.

Exposure - Any property near a fire that may catch fire itself because of the transfer of heat or burning material from the main fire.

Fire Engine - See Apparatus.

Fire House - self explanatory; where the fire engines and the firemen live and work. And by the way, Boston firehouses are not called fire stations.

Fire Alarm or Fire Alarm Office (FAO) - situated and isolated at #59 The Fenway in the otherwise heavily populated Fenway section of Boston. And, yes, it's rather close to Fenway Park. It looks like a fort. The people who work inside are the ones who send the fire engines to the fires and anywhere else they have to go. They call themselves "The Eye That Never Closes."

First alarm - the initial alarm transmitted to the fire houses by the Fire Alarm Office. Generally, the assignment was 3 engine companies, 2 ladder companies, and a district chief. In some areas of the city, a rescue is also dispatched while, in even fewer instances, a deputy chief is dispatched.

Halligan Bar or Halligan Tool - Called simply "The Halligan," this is a multipurpose tool used for tasks ranging from forced entry to overhaul. The tool was designed by Deputy Chief Hugh Halligan of the New York Fire Department in 1948. It weighs about 8 pounds and is about 32-inches in length. Owing to the idiosyncrasies of New York laws - because the Halligan was designed by a member - the New York Fire Department was not able to purchase and use the first commercially available tools. That distinction belongs to the Boston Fire Department. (You're welcome, chief.)

Heavy Stream Appliances - A heavy stream appliance is a stationary, portable or elevated water delivery appliance through which large amounts of water are delivered upon a fire. Often called "deck guns," owing to their placement on top on engine companies. They are often seen as the appliance of choice when an interior attack is impossible to make.

Inch-and-a-half line - a length of fire hose, usually 200 to 250-feet long, consisting of 50-foot lengths of hose, 1½-inches in diameter and coupled together. This is the hose most commonly used for an interior attack when speed is more important than having large quantities of water.

Inch-and-three-quarters line - a length of fire hose, usually 200 to 250-feet long, consisting of 50-foot lengths of hose, 1¾-inches in diameter and coupled together. This is now the most preferred hose because it essentially replaces the inch and a half line - it provides a lot more water and is much easier to maneuver than a 2 and one half inch line.

Ladder Company - The fire engine with the ladders. Usually equipped with a 100 or 110-foot aerial ladder and ground ladders of varying heights; from 16 to 50-feet. These guys are the ones who perform the initial search and rescue operations at a fire. They also perform open-up, ventilation, and overhauling operations. It is safe to say that the job of an engine company would be much, much more difficult without good ladder companies facilitating their fast attack operations.

Overhauling - the phase of fire ground operations that takes place after visible fire has been extinguished. It usually commences when certain firemen are assigned to pull down walls and ceilings, looking for hidden pockets of fire. It is a very labor intensive function.

Patrol Desk - area in a fire house where all official communications are centered. The patrol desk is usually a smallish area near the front of the fire house. It is manned 24/7 by the firemen working on a tour of duty.

Rake - A long wooden pole with a steel hook on one end. It is used almost exclusively to tear down ceilings and walls during overhauling operations.

Rescue Company - Usually a large, box-type fire engine that carries heavy tools. In addition to regular fire-ground duties when so ordered, the guys assigned to a rescue company generally use their tools to perform collapses.

Stick - another name for an aerial ladder. It came into being when ladders were made of wood.

Tillerman - the fireman who drives the back end

of a tractor-trailer type ladder truck. And yes, it's just as much fun as you think it is.

Tour of Duty - Between 1963 and 1983, a day tour of duty began at 8:00 AM and ended at 6:00 PM. A night tour began at 6:00 PM and ended at 8:00 AM. The department has since implemented a schedule calling for 24-hour tours of duty.

Tower Ladder - The fire engine with the bucket on the end of the ladder. In other municipalities, it is often referred to as a platform ladder truck. The guys assigned here will respond to alarms in their regular areas and function as a regular ladder truck. They are available for all special calls where their particular type of apparatus is needed.

Working Fire - a fire large enough to require some additional help but not large enough to warrant the striking of a second or greater alarm. The additional help sent usually consisted of one engine company, one rescue company and the division commander, i.e., a Deputy Chief. In 2007, the department eliminated the working fire designation and forced fire ground commanders to order a second alarm if they wanted any extra help.

We Did It Our Way

Unofficially, the war years began in 1963. The fires came more and more frequently. The running increased. A lot. Where once a company that responded 2000 times was considered very busy, the war years would push them down toward the bottom half of the list. For the next twenty-one years, Boston's jakes would run crazy and go to more fires than ever; in short, we were, as the title suggests, busy as hell.

At that time it all began, the Boston Fire Department was still using many pieces of fire apparatus that had been purchased in the early to late 1940s. There were a smattering of pumps and ladder trucks purchased in 1962 and 1963. Each piece of apparatus was of the open cab design. There were no jump seats or crew cabs. Hosemen rode the back step of hose wagons and pumps, laddermen rode on the side of tiller trucks outfitted with wooden aerial ladders.

Beyond the obvious disadvantages of riding on open apparatus - inclement weather - another issue charged to the forefront when, in June 1967, the city of Boston was shaken by riots. Suddenly, firemen became the targets of demonstrators and rioters; they were bombarded with rocks, bricks, and anything that wasn't nailed down. Then, on June 3, the widespread lawlessness dragged the city into a near-deadly spiral - a fire lieutenant from Ladder 4 was shot and wounded by a sniper after answering a false alarm. Witnesses said that as many as ten rounds had been fired.

Clearly, something had to be done - and fast.

So, armed with piles of angle iron and plexiglass, the maintenance men got straight to work and outfitted each fire engine - beginning with those in the riot areas - with a crude form of protection. They built square frames from the angle iron - large enough to fit over the front seat and the back step and small enough (they looked like telephone booths) to fit on the side of ladder companies. After they welded the square angle-iron frames to the apparatus, they finished the job by attaching plexiglass to cover the frames. It wasn't pretty but it provided some protection.

At about the same time, the department began sending a reduced assignment to pulled street boxes. Before the riots, when a fire box was pulled, the Fire Alarm Office would transmit the alarm and the first three engines and two ladders companies would respond. When reduced assignments were in effect, the alarms were no longer transmitted over the airways and into the fire houses. Instead, the first due engine and truck would be contacted by telephone and sent to investigate.

Engine 24 and its new riot shields.

With the benefit of 20/20 hindsight, it is easy to see how the riots were a quasi coming of age for the Boston Fire Department. The romance was finally stripped from the profession. Gone from the public conscious was the derring-do fireman with the haughty attitude hanging onto the side of a rickety old ladder truck as he and his mates sped by and likely waved to the cheering bystanders who lined the sidewalks - and in more cases than not, wished it was they who were aboard as well. Where once the newspapers painted firemen with an admiring and dutiful brush, and called them "fire laddies," the grand coverage now stopped. Yes, they continued to write stories about fires; it's the pedestal that vanished.

In 1968, the city purchased the first closed fire engines - American LaFrance ladder trucks and Ward LaFrance pumps. Fourteen Hahn pumps were purchased in 1970 and, so, became the first pumps equipped with 5-inch front suctions and air horns. In 1976, Seagrave ladder trucks and Ward LaFrance pumps became the first of the crew cab design used in Boston.

With the influx of new fire apparatus, the department gradually eliminated double-unit engine companies (hose wagon and pump) and replaced them with single-unit (pump only) companies. This was possible because of the introduction of 400 gallon booster tanks in 1962 and 1968, followed in 1970 by the introduction of 500-gallon tanks on the Hahn pumps. The advantages were immediately obvious.

Until then, with a few exceptions, Boston's pumps and hose wagons carried only 150 gallons of water. In almost all instances, while a double-unit waited for the pump to connect to the hydrant and charge a line, they would use the booster line on the hose wagon to attack the fire. Sure, you can put out some fire with a booster line but clearly not as much as with a larger hose. Some engine companies carried high pressure booster lines and while they were certainly useful, they didn't compare to the larger line.

On a single-unit engine company however, this additional capacity in the booster tank allowed the pump operator to charge the inch-and-a-half attack line first and then connect the feeder line to the pump. There was no waiting for water - unless, of course, you were running two-and-a-half inch line. (The pump operator never charged a big line without receiving an order from his boss. The reasons were obvious: at 65-pounds per 50-foot length, the line is cumbersome enough when it's empty. When you add water, you also add 105-pounds per 50-foot length. Now accept that the average stretch may be up to 200-feet. Translation? 200-feet of big line weighs 260 pounds when it's empty and 680 pounds when it's charged. Unless you're running with an officer and ten men, you wait for the boss to give the order to fill the line.

Therefore, where once you had to try and hold a fire in check with a booster line while you waited for the pump to be connected, now, with 400 gallons of water and an inch-and-a-half line in your arsenal, you could attack the fire and, with any luck, put a lot of it out. Of course, this system worked much better in the smaller, three-story frame homes in Boston's various neighborhoods. But, as we learned in the introduction, that's where about two-thirds of the fires were.

Those of us who worked in those engine companies were lucky indeed. We were the beneficiaries of the slam-dunk expertise of the officers in command. We watched and learned. And we followed, too. Because those guys led from the front. They wouldn't have it any other way. These officers - and I have to name them because they were that good - were all Lieutenants at the time: Joe Germano, Paul Callaghan, Eddie Kenney, Eddie Paris, Jack Force, Bill Shea, and Les Monarch.

Now I'm positive that similar leaders had an identical effect on firemen in other companies. This means that the officer corps was very strong everywhere, not just where we worked. To a man, they were strong, confident leaders whose approach was straightforward yet simple. Our engine company bosses would size up the situation in a hurry. Though never specifically stated or written, we learned the basic tenets of single-unit engine company operations from our leaders:

Get out of the fire house and fast!

Get your own water.

Drop a feeder or (beginning in 1970) use the front suction.

When in doubt, drop two feeders.

Run a line.

Charge it immediately.

They all knew how much hose we needed to get where we needed to go and there was never any time wasted in asking for, and then waiting for, the water. As the pump rolled to a stop in front of a fire building, the officer would give the driver a simple set of orders: "Break the line at XXX feet and charge it." That's all there was to it. They made the decision and they were almost always right. I can count on the fingers of one hand the number of times they misjudged the amount of hose we needed - it was always that they decided on running 50-feet too much.

Now, here's a surprise, one of the keys to the success of this method was that we did not have our attack lines pre-connected. Why did that make a difference? Because the tendency is almost always to take the whole line - if you have 300-feet laying in a hose bed and it's pre-connected, you'll usually just start dragging hose to the fire without giving any consideration to how the extra hose can render your attack line almost useless - it will be filled with kinks. You'll have more hose laying in the street than inside the building where the fire is.

Single-unit operations, proficient line company fire officers, larger booster tanks, when combined with a motivated crew - well, the standard was set. I can say with all candor and certainty that there were thousands of times when Boston's engine companies put water - lots of it - on a fire within forty-five to sixty seconds of the pump rolling to a stop and its air brake being set.

While the tactical transformation of Boston's engine companies ambled along, ladder company operations remained pretty much the same. The major change was in the transition from wooden ladders to metal ladders. The length of ground ladders was a constant; the length of aerial ladders increased from wooden 85-footers to metal 100-footers. With the purchase of closed cab ladder trucks in 1968, the department began to say goodbye to pompier ladders, the odd-looking though rarely used gadget that is best defined by Wikipedia: A pompier ladder (from the French word "pompier," meaning firefighter) is a type of ladder that can be attached to a window sill or similar ledge by the use of a hooked extending bill with serrations on the underside. The hooked ladder then hangs suspended vertically down the face of the building. The ladder was developed to access buildings via enclosed alleys, lightwells and yards to which other types of ladder could not be taken. A pair of men and two ladders could be used to scale a building to considerable heights, by climbing from floor to floor and taking the ladders up behind and pitching to the next floor.

There were some old-time laddermen who had seen them used at a hotel in the Back Bay in the 1940s. Beyond that, the "pomps," as they were called, remained stored on ladder trucks gathering dust. However, every Boston jake had to climb those infernal things up to the sixth floor of a drill tower. Then, just for fun, before being accepted into the brotherhood, they made us hook our safety belts onto the goose-neck part of the ladder and lay back, arms spread. To my knowledge, everyone completed the exercise . . . and not one single man asked permission to do it again.

Tool-wise, the only addition to the ladder company's weapons was the adz, a building wreckers tool. It was introduced to the department by Jack Brignoli, of Ladder 7, the absolute artisan of demolition if one ever existed.

In discussing Boston's ladder companies, the need arises to explain something about our so-called "ladder culture," a nationally accepted reality. Just mention the Boston Fire Department and ladders in the same sentence and someone will say, "Boston is famous for their ladder work," or "The best ladder department ever," etc. However, my long asked and still unanswered question is, who said so? Hey, I don't dispute the legend - we added to it every time we threw a thirty-five - but where does this notion come from? Who started it? Who said it first? So far as I know, there isn't an answer. However, here's why we did what we did, a brief explanation about why we threw so many ladders during the war years.

Aerial ladders provide access to the roof - laddermen open roofs to ventilate buildings.

Ground ladders are raised to windows to rescue trapped people and/or to provide additional means of entrance and egress for engine companies.

Ladders aren't thrown for the hell of it, that's for sure. In fact, during what we call drill school, new recruits will spend a good portion of their training throwing and climbing ladders. It was excellent practice because after we went to our respective companies and started working a regular schedule, we spent a good deal of time doing both - throwing and climbing.

Boston is an old city. It wasn't laid out in grids like, say, Albuquerque or Phoenix. We don't have wide boulevards with tons of room. You've probably heard tales about Boston streets and how they're nothing but paved-over, former cow paths. Well, it's true. Our streets rarely run true north, south, east or west. (Imagine you're standing directly above a large bowl of spaghetti - that's the aerial view of Boston.) So it makes perfect sense to realize that with so many skinny-ass streets, it was often difficult to get even one ladder company close enough to use the aerial ladder, never mind the much desired two. Sometimes ground ladders were our only option and, so, the more the merrier. However, even when there was a "stick to the roof," ground ladders were always used. Nowadays, I suppose there are more technical (and contemporary) explanations our ladder culture but let me say this: we used lots of ladders because it was always better to have one raised and not need it than to need one and not have raised it. You just never knew where or when you'd need one. It was basic stuff for us....engine companies ran lines, ladder companies threw ladders.

All in all, the war years were a fun time to be a Boston fireman. There were bad days, of course, and there were worse days, but nothing more or less than what you'd expect from everyday life. I believe I speak for the overwhelming majority of those who were busy as hell and lived and worked that time, even a portion thereof, that we wouldn't trade the camaraderie and experiences for all the tea in China.

THE GREAT ESCAPE

"Bompo" hopped on to the back step of Engine 13's 1962 Ward LaFrance pump and rode from the fire house to a fire in a donut shop on Morrissey Boulevard, District 8.

He wasn't there very long before he fell off the top of a ladder and broke both ankles.

It had to hurt. It had to hurt a lot.

But, as is very often the case with fires in Boston, and the fire fighters who fight them, the situation started out routinely, quickly degenerated into something not so good and then, like magic, became an uproarious legend, a story for the ages.

After Bompo crumpled to the ground, clearly in agony, he was surrounded by fellow fire fighters from different companies. All wanted to help him. In a typical display, Bompo was gently tended to, probably had a cigarette shoved in his mouth - they did that in war movies and westerns, right? - and eventually rolled over on to a half-assed stretcher, and then, because there were only one or two city ambulances in Boston, unceremoniously maneuvered into the back of a police department station wagon and taken to Boston City Hospital, the BCH, a trip of some four miles. The hospital itself was (1) city-owned and operated and (2) located in a less-than-friendly, somewhat high crime South End neighborhood. As you will properly surmise, it was the hospital of choice for those who didn't otherwise have access to medical care. In other words, you didn't see very many people seeking care at the BCH if they had other alternatives - like stitching your own wound, for instance. The buildings, and there were many in the complex, were old and in dire need of a paint job, at least in the patient rooms. It was rife with long, dark corridors that connected different buildings and which, to some, functioned as secret passageways. God alone knows where they led.

When Bompo was admitted to the hospital, now sporting an ER-applied cast on each foot, he was placed in an open ward filled with various elements of mid-60s society; there were prisoners from local jails (those who feigned illness just to get out of their cell), drunks, crazy people, cry babies, and of course, the requisite stabbing and gunshot victims. In short, the BCH was no place for a self-respecting Boston fire fighter who had injured himself in the performance of his duties, no sir.

Entering our story from stage right is one Rodney Anthony Horton, an acutely aware man with a swagger in his step and a razor sharp intellect that would make Gillette proud. He was (and remains) a scarily bright, but, as those who know him say with amusement, a barely house broken friend of Bompo's. Rodney is a mental magician who can solve the strictest of problems with ease and often he sees simple solutions to awkward or complicated dilemmas that no one, not even Einstein, could envision. He borders on being a real-life Gyro Gearloose, one who was quite frequently too damned smart for his own good. When you consider a sliver of Rodney's childhood - his 3rd grade pronouncement that Emily Post and her rules of etiquette were "bullshit," an adult-like evaluation that landed his 8-year old butt in the principal's office - well, then you have all the ingredients for the opening pages of a book about the Boston Fire Department and its cast of characters. Like they say, he wasn't house broken.

Case in point: the morning after the fire at the Puritan Donut shop, after completing his night tour of duty on Ladder 23, Rodney went to visit Bompo in the hospital.

In less than thirty seconds after his arrival, the mental magician sized up the situation and decided that two broken ankles and the adjunct pain were quite enough inconvenience. Rodney was not about to let a member of Engine 13 - or any other Engine - endure this kind of purposeful torture at the hands of the dregs of society. There was no way in hell that his friend was going to stay in a hospital ward with a bunch of degenerate citizens who had decided, just for sport, to make enough noise, to raise enough ruckus, just enough to keep Bompo wide awake and miserable.

Rodney decided, on his own, that enough was enough. He would solve the problem by taking Bompo to another hospital. He didn't quite know how he was going to do it, but he knew he would figure it out. And why not? Didn't he always figure it out? (Yes, he did.)

Telling Bompo he'd be right back, Rodney called a friend who, as luck would have it, was one of two ambulance drivers at the BCH. Laying out the plans for his ambulance-driver friend, he found a willing participant in what can only be described as a plot to kidnap a patient and transport him to another hospital, one more fitting his station in life - the Carney Hospital in Dorchester.

So, they snuck upstairs, entered the open ward, and without much effort and zero fanfare, just wheeled Bompo out the door, down the corridor, into the elevator, and finally, when they hit the first floor, simply picked Bompo up, placed him in the ambulance and took off. Within fifteen minutes, they rolled into the parking lot at the Carney Hospital. Rodney went inside and told the ER people what was going on. Well, the ER people told him that there was no way they would treat a patient who had already been treated ... someone who already had a cast on each ankle!

Rodney was shocked and pissed that the ER people refused to accept Bompo as a patient. This was not good. They'd already done the hard part, kidnapping the patient, and now they were being told that they were being refused treatment? But fear not because remember I told you that Rodney was a mental magician who could solve the strictest of problems with ease and often saw solutions to problems that no one, not even Einstein, could envision?

Well, here he stood, ready to prove the analysis correct.

Drum roll please ...

With Bompo still in the ambulance, Rodney and his partner in crime drove to the nearest hardware store. Rodney purchased a package of hacksaw blades and there, right there in the back of the ambulance, sawed both casts off of Bompo's ankles. Then they drove back to the ER and demanded they accept him.

They did.

Of course, the story didn't end there. Nope.

Within twenty-four hours, Rodney was summoned to the Fire Commissioner's office to answer for his crime. He arrived in the requisite full dress uniform.

Now you have to know a little about the headquarters building. It's a drab looking, three-story, yellow brick edifice that sits at 115 Southampton

Street in Roxbury. But, structure aside, its what's inside HQ that has been known to send shivers up the spines of fire fighters and all others who had been so summoned.

It's filled with brass!

With big shots!

From end to end, from stem to stern – there's brass everywhere!

Unknown to many at this early stage of his career, though, Rodney has another side to him. He doesn't give a double damn about gold and silver and even less about the opinions or pronouncements (or both) of those who wear it.

And, so, while he was standing tall in the Commissioner's office, with fingers waving in his face, he didn't raise his voice, he just politely told the fire commissioner that he didn't give two shits what he thought or believed because to him, to Rodney, it was simple: his friend was in trouble and well, dammit, he'd do the same thing all over again if a similar situation presented itself.

Of course, there wasn't anything the department could really do about the incident. So when their intimidation tactics didn't work, they dismissed him with a warning - don't do it again.

Yeah, right. They had a better chance of winning the Power Ball jackpot every Wednesday and Saturday for six months running that they had of exorcising Rodney's maverick propensities.

Whiskey as Legal Tender

There was a bakery on Clifton Street in Roxbury that made the best eclairs this side of heaven. In fact, there are those who would argue that the bakers in heaven had nothing on the Roxbury crowd. Jam packed with custard like you read about; these oblong treasures were covered in the richest chocolate icing known to man. Every afternoon or evening, just as their night tour got going, say, between four and five o'clock, the gang from Group 3 on Ladder 4 would drive down to Clifton Street and wait in the parking lot while one of their members - a friend of the bakery's security guard - went inside the building. Those who stood by outside never had more than five minutes to wait before the purveyor-in-chief to emerge from the bakery carrying two trays filled with forty-eight mouth-watering eclairs. Then he would carefully place them in the front seat bedside the Lieutenant who willingly assumed command of their well-being. "Protect those with your life!" the firemen shouted out to the boss.

Of course, as you may well surmise, it was close to impossible to drive all the way back to the fire house without sampling their treasure, the facts of which answer at least one burning question: Yes, it is possible to tiller a ladder truck with one hand while eating an eclair with the other. On another note, almost as if by heavenly decree, just to prove that the Fire Gods are genuine entities, Ladder 4 never had a run on their way back to quarters.

If you consider the average complement for this fire house, housing an engine and ladder company, there were usually eight to ten firemen working every night this happened. Translation: Forty-eight eclairs divided by eight or ten, well, you do the math.

Of course, they wouldn't be consumed all in one sitting. I have it on good authority that for the year or so that the bakery deal went on, there was nothing like coming back from a fire and after trudging up the stairs to the second floor kitchen, pouring a hot cup of coffee and devouring yet another sampling of eclair magic. (During the year in question, my good authority also tells me that a certain member of Group 4, the group that always relieved Group 3 in the morning, used to come in extra early in the hope that there would be an eclair left over. He once admitted that the morning he found two eclairs was one of the best days of his fire department life.)

Of course, everyone understood that such a treat deserved first-class reciprocity. So the first Christmas after the eclair bonanza began, the crew drove to the bakery armed with a gallon of top-shelf spirits. It was a small price to pay - exceptionally small they believed.

They drove into the parking lot as always. The main man walked through a door in the back of the building, carrying the gallon of booze by the handle. Just then, a police car from Division 2, the police station right across the square from their fire house, drove into the parking lot. The firemen watched with interest as a cop got out of the car, went to the back, opened the trunk and removed a case of booze, placed it on his shoulder and walked through the same back door.

Within three minutes, the fireman emerged carrying two racks of eclairs. He placed the bounty in the jump seat and climbed back aboard the ladder truck.

They were curious because this was the first time they'd ever seen cops at the bakery before. So, they decided to wait a minute before leaving.

Their curiosity was satisfied when the cop emerged carrying four racks of eclairs! All of which verifies that long-held notion that whiskey can be and is legal tender.

Fire College

Every year, all Boston Lieutenants and Captains attend something called Fire College. It's a time for the HQ desk commanders to tell us what we already know and, on rare occasions, to share their latest revelation. One such meeting was filled with a discussion about a new piece of equipment we may (or may not) be using in the future. A HQ fixture, a Captain, stepped forward with a brand new nozzle the department was considering for purchase. It was a state of the art appliance that, get this, operated by radio frequency - that's right, the flow of water through the nozzle tip was regulated by a radio signal. The Captain was unable to conceal his excitement over this new gadget. He was almost giddy as he explained how it worked. Then someone in the back of the room, a young Lieutenant as it was, raised his hand.

"You have a question?" the HQ Captain gushed.

"Yes, Cap, I do. What about fires in cellars? My portable radio won't work in a cellar because of, I think, the RF attenuation. Won't the same thing be true with that nozzle?"

Several heads nodded in agreement.

"It shouldn't be a problem."

There are quizzical looks all around.

"But it could be, right? I mean if I can't use my portable radio below grade . . . isn't the same thing going on? The nozzle might not work, right? I could lose my water, right?"

Captains and Lieutenants, old and new, are on the edges of their seats, waiting.

"It's unlikely. Probably not."

Looks of disbelief spread across the room.

"But it could happen, right? I mean, Cap, if we're heading down a flight of cellar stairs to attack a fire and all of a sudden we lose our radio signal . . . we'll lose out water, too. Right?"

This time, everyone is nodding in agreement.

And the HQ Captain replied …

Wait for it …

"Well, if the radio frequency is lost and you lose your water, you can just move around a little bit until you get the frequency connection back."

"Move around?" the young lieutenant asked. "Let me get this straight. You're saying that if I'm in a burning cellar and we lose our water because of this radio controlled nozzle, all we have to do is move around?"

"Yes, just until you get the signal back."

"Cap, I haven't been on the job as long as you but let me tell you, if I'm in a burning cellar and I lose my water, I'm pretty well screwed. The idea that we can just move around until we get our water back is ridiculous."

"Well, the department wants to test them and see how they perform in field tests."

A loud chorus of groans greeted the captain's response.

Finally, from the middle of the room, an old-time Lieutenant, a guy with thirty-five years on the job piped in, "Well, Cap, with all due respect, you put one of those pieces of shit on my company to test, the only thing it will get is a swimming test 'cause I'm throwing it in Boston fuckin' Harbor."

Well now, so much for *that* nozzle.

There's No Such Thing A Free Lunch . . . On Second Thought

As the sun rose on the fire house, there were two very tired firemen sitting at a ten-foot long table in the kitchen playing Gin Rummy. It had been a very busy night. The firemen had gone to three tough fires in the past fourteen hours. The remainder of the crew was laying down upstairs waiting for their reliefs to arrive so they could go home and get some sleep.

At just before 7:00 AM, the truck captain walked into the kitchen. He was a bit beyond his years for service in a busy, busy fire house and as it turned out, was not very far from being felled by the heart attack that would end his career.

The captain was also a creature of some predictable habit. He always arrived at the same time, always put his lunch - ham and cheese sandwich and a Twinkie - in the refrigerator, walked upstairs to his office and locker, changed into his work uniform, and came back down to the kitchen to have his first cup of coffee.

Today would be the same.

Well, almost the same.

"Good morning, men. Busy night?" the captain asked.

Busy as Hell

"Hi, Cap. Same as usual. Busy as hell," one of the rummy players replied.

The captain nodded, put his brown bag in the refrigerator and as he opened the door to leave, he met another fireman on his way into the kitchen. They exchanged pleasantries as they passed.

The newly arrived fireman got a cup, walked to the corner of the room, filled the cup with freshly brewed coffee and sat, heavily.

"Hungry, Ray?" one of the rummy players asked.

"Hell, I'm starved," Ray replied.

"I left my lunch from last night. It's in the fridge. I'm not going to eat it. Ham and cheese and a Twinkie. Help yourself."

"Damn, thanks," Ray replied as he got up, opened the refrigerator door, found the brown bag, sat back down, and began to enjoy his bounty.

About half-way through the second half of his sandwich, the captain came back into the kitchen. He got a cup of coffee and sat down at the long kitchen table, directly across from Ray. At precisely the same time, one of the rummy players suddenly tossed his cards on the table and made a bee line for the door. He went outside the kitchen, stopped, stood quietly, and just listened.

Ray finished the sandwich.

Then he picked up the Twinkie and started to open

it.

The explosion came.

"Goddammit, Ray, what are you doing eating my lunch!?" the captain bellowed.

Poor Ray. He'd been had. Big time.

He stuttered and stammered and tried to explain.

The captain seethed.

He was pissed!

But, then Ray said the magic words, the name that explained everything.

"But Cap, Fast Eddie," he began.

The captain put his hand up.

Ray stopped talking.

"Fast Eddie gave it to you?" the captain asked.

"Yes," Ray replied with visible relief.

The captain charged out of the kitchen and went to the PA system.

"Felson, get your ass down to the main floor!"

Felson, who had run and hid behind the opposite side of the ladder truck, came walking, and very sheepishly so, back to the scene of the crime. The captain was standing there, hands on hips and loaded for bear, waiting.

But it's a funny thing about Ol' Fast Eddie.

He had this personality and smile that just melted the captain.

It was impossible to stay angry with him.

And Fast Eddie knew it.

"Sorry, Cap, I just couldn't resist. I saw the chance to prank Ray and I took it. Here, let me buy you lunch," he offered, extracting a five-dollar bill from his pocket.

Predictably, at least to Fast Eddie, the Captain laughed, took the five bucks and said, "Helluva prank. It worked, too. He was scared shitless."

Okay, fast forward about six months:

As the sun rose on the fire house, there were two very tired firemen sitting at a ten-foot long table in the kitchen playing Gin Rummy. It had been a very busy night. The firemen had gone to three tough fires in the past fourteen hours. The remainder of the crew was laying down upstairs waiting for their reliefs to arrive so they could go home and get some sleep.

At just before 7:00 AM, the truck captain walked into the kitchen. He was a bit beyond his years for service in a busy, busy fire house and as it turned out, was not very far from being felled by the heart attack that would end his career.

Now if this story sounds familiar, well, it should.

Yes, it is a duplication of the first two paragraphs.

And why is that, you ask?

Because, believe it or not, Felson pulled the exact same prank on the exact same Captain and the exact same Ray only six months later.

Hey, they didn't call him Fast Eddie for nothing.

Made In Italy

Legend has it that the Fire Alarm Office was once outfitted with a newfangled digital-type clock/calendar. You remember when those first appeared, right? They were wonderful inventions. Now we didn't have to look at the hands on a clock or a watch and decide what time is was. The newfangled clock told us the time. The exact time. It was no longer, "Almost six-thirty," it was now "Six twenty-seven."

The fire alarm guys probably loved their new digital clock because they are required to end every transmission by stating the time. What can possibly be easier than looking up at a new clock and reading a few numbers?

But, this clock was a bit different. It wasn't made in Japan, or Taiwan. In fact, it had a little label on the bottom that said, and I assume, proudly, Made In Italy. Hey, what do you know? It was something from Italy that didn't have spaghetti sauce or pepperoni all over it. So, it was no surprise that said new clock was noticed and embraced by one of the more Italian members of the fire alarm office, a man who's last name ended in an East Boston vowel.

Let's fast forward to New Year's Eve. I'm not sure what year it was but will guess that is was 1971 going on 1972. Anyway, the gang working that night were gathered around, anxiously waiting for midnight so they could watch the clock switch to January 1 and usher in the new year with a nice Italian flair.

Our Italian fire alarm friend stood front and center.

He was excited.

Finally, the moment of truth was upon them.

The midnight time signal beeped.

Happy New Year!

The clock.

The Made in Italy clock.

Switched to:

December 32, 1971.

Bellflower Street

Friday, May 22, 1964, was a very important day in my life. Little did I know that it would become one of my life's most eventful days, and now, almost fifty years later, it remains so.

The day began when I arrived at the Marine Corps recruiting office on D Street in South Boston at nine o'clock in the morning (okay, 0900) where, along with a few other similarly inclined youngsters seventeen years of age and a bit older, I listened to the recruiter tell us what life would be like in the Marines. We watched a black-and-white film about the Marines and their WWII battles, took a few tests, filled out a million forms and, generally, congratulated ourselves for taking the first step toward following in our father's collective footsteps.

Many of those in attendance had their actual enlistment delayed so they could enjoy a summer vacation before heading south, to Parris Island, South Carolina. I wasn't one of them. My official enlistment - when they owned me officially, when I took my oath, would occur the following Friday, May 29, precisely 24 years after my father had taken his oath and joined these same Marines in 1940. Spurning the notion of taking the summer off, my commitment would begin only fourteen days later, on June 5 which, as it turned out, was less than a full day after I was scheduled to graduate from high school on June 4. As I recounted many times in later years, I graduated at 2 o'clock on the 4th and twenty-two hours later, on the 5th at noon, I left.

So, when all the preliminaries were completed and after some well wishes from the recruiter, Sergeant Reilly -- he probably laughed like hell and thought, "You'll be sorrrry." - we were dismissed.

I had borrowed the family car - a blue-on-blue '58 Chevy Bel Air - to keep my appointment and by pre-arrangement, would drive to Engine 43's quarters and meet my father where he was working the day tour, although in a different capacity this day; he was driving Car 12 for Captain Bob Regan who was the acting District Chief. Arriving at just after noon, I expected to hang around until Dad was relieved and he drove us home. We sat in the kitchen and drank coffee while I filled him in on what happened at the recruiter's office. A few of the firemen from Engine 43 and Ladder 20 came in and wished me luck, firemen I had known for many years, since the days I used to ride the (now Red Line) subway train from Shawmut Station four stops to Andrew Square to deliver my father's dinner. It was a fun day. So much to look forward to - so much to anticipate.

Then, as history will later record, the so-called "inside phone," the direct hot line from Fire Alarm to the fire house, rang at 1:38 pm.

The man who was standing watch - the house patrol - listened to what the man on the other end was telling him, and, as he did, scribbled an address on the small piece of blackboard that was secured to the desk top. At almost the same instant, he jammed the toggle switch downward and set off the house alarm: Woooop Woooop Woooop Woooop

"Truck only! Ladder 20 only! 26 Bellflower Street! Striking 7251!"

As the drama quickly unfolded in the fire house on Massachusetts Avenue, a sister act was being performed at the fire house on Columbia Rod where Engine 21 had received identical instructions: Go to 26 Bellflower Street.

In clock life, a minute later, at 1:39 pm, but it was really at the same time, the fire house bells erupted to life with their clanging, Morse code sounding alert, the eternal summons:

••••••• •• •••••• •

Sensing the urgency when the phone call preceded the alarm bells, Engine 43's crew had already saddled up and were right on Ladder 20's tail as they flew out the door.

Engine 1 and Ladder 7's crews were doing the same thing in different fire houses. They were the remainder of the first alarm assignment.

My father and I walked toward the patrol desk. Just then, the pay phone in the lobby rang. I still don't know why I did it, but I walked over and answered it, "Hello."

There was a frantic woman on the other end. "Is Paul O'Keefe there?!" she screamed.

"No," I answered, "he just went out the door on a run."

"There's a fire near our house on Dorset Street," she screamed, "hurry!"

I ran to my father and told him about the woman on the phone. He yelled, "Let's go!" and took off toward the rear of the fire house.

Just before we reached the back door that leads to the parking area, we could see everything through the big group of side windows that faced onto Glynn Way.

The black smoke was already covering the bright blue sky.

It was stunning, beyond belief!

Just then, Lieutenant Jimbo Kennedy's voice came in loud and clear as he reported to Fire Alarm, "Second alarm!" he ordered, unable to conceal the urgency in his voice.

Dad ran inside the maintenance shop and yelled loudly for Captain Regan who was showing the maintenance area to a US Army reserve friend of his. Having heard the second alarm ordered, the Captain was already on his way. He appeared immediately, took one look out through the wide open garage doorway and repeated the call, "Let's go!"

Captain Regan said goodbye to his friend and motioned for me to get inside the chief's car ... guess I was going to the fire, huh?

Dad put the key into the ignition and . . . nothing.

He turned it again . . . still nothing.

Dead battery.

In an instant, Captain Regan jumped out of the car and pointing at me, yelled to his friend, "Take him to the fire, will ya?!"

"Wait!" Dad yelled as he ran to the back of the car, opened the trunk and handed me his Engine 43 helmet and dungaree jacket. "Take these," he said, knowingly, "you're gonna need them. And for God's sake, be careful! Now go!"

I climbed into the Captain's friend's car - and why do I still remember that it was a Ford Thunderbird? - and just as we started to pull out of the driveway, Dad suddenly appeared at the open side window. He wordlessly handed me, almost tossed, a pair of his

Knapp work shoes through the open passenger window.

I looked at his feet.

White socks.

No shoes.

And just like that - Zoooom! - off we went.

For me, inside, the excitement was growing, intensifying; to this very day, I believe it was at this very moment that I decided what I wanted to do with my life.

By now, I learned later on, the third and fourth alarms had also been requested and transmitted, and in an unprecedented fashion for District Chief Bob Greene of District 6 had ordered Fire Alarm to "Strike the third and fourth alarms."

Captain Regan's friend drove right at the fire. He turned from Glynn Way and on to Southampton Street, headed for Andrew Square. Then he quickly turned toward the fire, turning onto the service road near Howard Johnson's and then onto the off-ramp that went behind the old Russell Boiler Works on Boston Street.

When we reached the corner and just as started to turn left, toward Andrew Square, away from the fire, he told me that this was where I had to get out. I was no more than a couple of blocks from the fire when he wished me luck, bid me farewell, and made his getaway. I don't know how he ever got out of that burgeoning traffic jam, and the only thing I had to prove he did was that he returned my dress shoes some time later.

So here I am, out of the car.

You can imagine what it was like, can't you?

The scene was utter chaos.

It was electric!

It was happening less than 500-feet away.

I took off toward the fire, running as fast as my legs would carry me.

There were people everywhere.

Some were standing like statues, staring.

Scores were running away from the fire.

Scores more were running toward it.

Immense tongues of orange fire crackled above the rooftops.

The sky was filled with a black, bubbly, liquid-looking smoke.

You could actually hear the fire roar!

And there were sirens.

Millions of sirens.

The old-fashioned mechanical type.

They were coming from everywhere.

They multiplied the urgency.

And, of course, there were fire engines.

They were surrounding the area.

Busy as Hell

It seemed like they were coming up from underground.

From my on-the-run vantage point, approaching the corner of Boston and Bellflower Streets, there were fire engines arriving from the only two directions available, up from Andrew Square, down from Edward Everett Square.

So what does a 17-year old kid do now?

Help, I guess.

By now, and I only presume this time line, Deputy Chief Fred Clauss, arrived on Bellflower Street and immediately ordered the fifth alarm. Then, within another seven minutes, he ordered an additional five engine companies, and then, finally, in what must have sounded like a desperate move, he ordered "all possible help" be sent to the fire that right this instant lay before my wide and wondering eyes.

Drawing ever closer to the chaos on display farther up Boston Street, I was pulling my dungaree jacket on and looking for some kind of clue about what to do. I was self-conscious because, well, you see, I had an Engine 43 helmet on my head and while I doubted that anyone would much care about checking my birth certificate before thinking I should be helping - hey, I looked like a real fireman, right? - I was still a 17-year old kid terribly afraid of making a mistake and making Engine 43 look bad. Then I made it to the corner of

Boston and Bellflower Streets.

I stood statue-like; stunned, mesmerized.

Dear God in heaven, can't anyone stop this?

My eyes were overwhelmed.

The fire was mammoth.

The houses looked small.

Tiny.

I could see nothing more.

Just the scene before me.

And the heat was intense.

I put my hand to my face and felt.

My skin was hot.

Four of my five senses were on high alert.

The fifth, taste, was trying.

Can you taste a fire storm?

I watched the firemen, scrambling around, dragging hose.

I knew what they were doing but I had no idea what to do.

Then, a miracle.

Jimbo Kennedy.

For all who knew him or had the pleasure of working with James D. Kennedy, they all say the same thing. He was the best. God didn't make many men like Jimbo Kennedy. My father worked with him for many years and thought the world of him. In fact, when I needed a sponsor for my Confirmation a few years earlier, in 1959 - someone to sign an official Catholic form saying I was deserving - well, Dad asked Jimbo to sign. He did. Jimbo also proved that he knew what he was doing. He ordered his driver to ditch the ladder truck on the dead-ended West Bellflower Street, out of the way of the engine companies.

So now, here I am, standing on the edge of Hell, at the corner of Boston and Bellflower, all dressed up like a real live fireman but with absolutely no clue about what to do next. My brain screamed "Help them, you idiot!"

But I didn't know how.

Suddenly, I snapped out of my trance when Jimbo Kennedy grabbed my arm and ordered, "Mike, find an engine company to help and get to work!"

Message received.

So, stripped of all my youthful indecision, I immediately reached down and started trying to help drag a 2½-inch line toward one of the buildings on the right side, the even side, of Bellflower Street. I had no idea which engine company the hose belonged to, and I suppose at this point it didn't matter. I found out real quick that dragging hose wasn't as easy as it looked. Each 50' length of hose weighed about 65 pounds; when it was filled with water, as these were, it weighed 170 pounds; there were as many as six or seven 50' lengths connected together, making the task extremely difficult.

Struggling to pull with all my might, I remained self conscious about being dressed like a fireman and even more concerned about the number 43 on my helmet.

Would anyone question me?

Out me as a total impostor?

Well, it didn't take this 17-year old very long to realize that I could have been dressed in a Santa Claus suit and no one would have given a double damn. Just so long as I dragged hose.

I heard someone yell. "Hey!"

When I looked around, he was waving his arm like a third-base coach sending the runner home. "More line!" he yelled.

Then, just as I turned back toward Boston Street to comply with the new order, I felt an incredible blast of heat on my back. I somehow had the good sense (self preservation, no doubt) not to turn around and, instead, ran away from its source.

I got probably ten feet away before turning back to see ... the fire had jumped the street!

Buildings that were, not ten seconds ago, seemingly safe and secure were now fully ablaze. I could only see the first house on the left side of Bellflower Street. The rest were gone; the fire storm had devoured them and moved on, looking for more homes to gobble up and destroy.

BUSY AS HELL

BELLFLOWER STREET BURNING

It found them.

The 43 on my borrowed helmet aside, I stayed with these firemen for a long while as they jockeyed the line back and forth and all around, trying to make a dent. At some point, we wound up on the second floor rear porch with a 2 ½-inch line, doing our best to keep the fire away. If you look at the pictures, you'll see a light colored three-decker on the left, just in from Boston Street. That's where we were. No one asked me who I was or what I was doing there. No one asked me why I wasn't with my company, Engine 43. In fact, at one point, one of the firemen actually told me to take a turn on the nozzle. Tentatively, I agreed.

It felt heavy in my hand as I leaned it on the porch railing but at least I was able to figure out how to open the thing ... move the handle in the opposite direction from where it was now, when it was closed.

I doubtless gave myself away when I gave the handle a good yank towards me and felt the sudden surge in back pressure as it damn near knocked me on my ass. But they didn't seem to mind. In their eyes, I was a kid fireman who probably had never seen anything like this before or, as I now believe, they recognized me for precisely what I was and figured that if I was crazy enough to be there, well, they may as well put me to work.

Eventually, the fire-fighting effort had been reduced to a fairly academic exercise. The basic tenants of fire-ground effectiveness had been realized and from a tactical point of view, the fire had gone through three very different stages: (1) locate the fire, (2) confine it, (3) put it out.

As you may suspect, finding the fire was never a

problem. This means that the primary fire-ground efforts were centered in a very aggressive effort to confine the fire and, so, to protect the neighboring homes, called "the exposures" in fire-ground jargon. This was not an easy task, and for more than a few harrowing moments, there was a very real concern that a firestorm was imminent, a situation where a fire of this size and magnitude reaches such ferocity that it creates and sustains its own wind system and could, would, literally overwhelm the immediate area and race all the way to Andrew Square, consuming hundreds of homes in its path.

The secondary phase was a professional mixture of aggressive and defensive tactics. Once the exposures were protected, the hundreds of firemen had all they could do to keep it confined. To highlight the genuine and immediate danger the fire chiefs dealt with, consider that there were over 250 roof fires reported in the area, every one caused by burning embers from the conflagration.

Finally, there was the "surround and drown phase," the time when the fire is very unlikely to extend beyond the buildings it has already consumed and the firemen just hold their ground, pouring tens of thousands of gallons of water every minute on whatever is left which, in the case of the fire on Bellflower Street, was an immense pile of wet and smoldering once-and-former three-deckers.

Some time later, when things had settled down a bit, I went looking for my father. I found him with Engine 43s crew; he had long since made his way over to the fire from the maintenance shop, the car battery replaced. We walked around a bit together, surveying the destruction. It was a very sobering sight, to think that over 300 people had lost their homes in a matter of minutes. Dad told me a funny story he had heard through the grapevine. Seems that Lieutenant John Campbell of Ladder 3, a well-known and very capable fire officer, did what every ladder officer did in those days when they arrived at a multiple alarm fire - they carried a 35-foot ladder with them. To John's credit, as they got closer, he told his guys to drop the ladder and get busy running lines to the fire. So, his Ladder 3 crew did just that; they dropped the ladder right there in the street and took off looking for fire hose to move.

I saw several people I knew; people who chased fires and fire engines in their spare time. Then Dad and I saw my little brother, Johnny, at the time a thirteen-year old junior high school kid who rode his bicycle from our house on Nixon Street to the fire - a 2½ mile trip through a traffic jam so large that many cars didn't move for hours-trapped as they were. Johnny told us that John "Buckeye" Glynn (actually, my little brother's Godfather) had put his bicycle in the front seat of Ladder 20 so it wouldn't get stolen while he watched the fire.

In truth, I have to confess, it was pretty cool being on Bellflower Street with an Engine 43 helmet on my head, playing fireman, and watching these jealous few friends of mine stare in amazement from far behind the fire lines, far away from the action.

Within the next hours, most of the buildings on the affected stretch of Bellflower Street and parts of Dorset Street had collapsed in and onto themselves. They were now just huge piles of burning rubble. It was an eerie scene similar to something you'd see on a WWII newsreel. So, like a lot of those in attendance, I decided that coffee would taste pretty good. I told my Dad I was going to walk down to Dorchester Avenue and get us both a cup from the Salvation Army truck.

Walking gingerly along the middle of Bellflower Street, navigating through the sea of fire engines parked at haphazard angles, and surveying the incredible damage farther down the street, I was feeling pretty good about myself. I thought I handled things pretty well, at least for someone who'd never fought a fire before. I also remembered that my fire department career would have to wait a while because in two short weeks I'd be off to Parris Island, South Carolina, where the Marines would show me a different kind of life style.

Then it happened.

Out of nowhere, she appeared.

A woman with a microphone.

Standing in front of a guy who had a huge camera set up on the street.

She stopped me.

I looked at her and she said, "Say hello to the Governor."

Endicott "Chub" Peabody, the 62nd Governor of Massachusetts and who, four months later, would lose his party's nomination for reelection, looked me dead in the eye and extended his hand.

So what do you do?

You shake his hand, that's what.

So far, so good.

I guess.

But, then he started to talk and ask me questions.

About the fire.

"I feel bad for the people who lost their houses," I somehow stammered, honestly.

About how young I looked.

"I was just appointed in January," I lied.

About where I was going.

"To get coffee for me and my father."

About how nice it was to meet me.

"Thank you."

Busy as Hell

See ya!

Thankfully, they didn't show my interview on TV. I'm guessing that they all knew I was lying through my teeth and besides, I didn't say anything worthwhile. Hey, I was just a kid!

But later that night, I saw the guy they chose to show on television.

He looked to be about 100 years old and was misidentified as Johnny Kelley. He wasn't a real fireman either but he was wearing a fire helmet just like me. Only his was red!

To his credit, though, he said it was the worst fire he'd seen in all his years.

Boston's jakes agreed, one and all.

NOTE: In a tragic twist of fate, Firefighters Frank Murphy of Engine 24 and Jim Sheedy of Ladder 4, were both admitted to the Boston City hospital, suffering from smoke inhalation while fighting the fire on Bellflower Street. A bit over four months later, both would be killed on Trumbull Street.

Mike Foley

The Aftermath of the
Bellflower Street Blaze

Make Believe Chief

While this story is about a make-believe chief - a firefighter who substituted for a chief one day - the reader has to know something about how the charade all came to be.

You see the real chief was one of the department's all-time characters. He was clearly the most irreverent fire chief any of us had ever met. He barked in the face of tradition and custom. He was the proverbial loose cannon rolling all over the decks of the USS BFD. Most other chiefs couldn't stand him because he wasn't one of them. He was everything a chief shouldn't be and nothing he should be.

By the time they've been promoted three times, most chief officers develop a certain presence. They're older and more mature. They've usually been on the job for at least twenty years and often many more. Most were family men with grown children, many in college. Many chiefs were grandfathers. Most of them were WWII veterans and knew how to wear a uniform.

But the chief we're talking about, well, he was different - very different. He was significantly overweight and hopelessly unkempt. He'd rarely tuck his shirt in. According to some of the chiefs he worked with, he was a slob. A messy office and chief's car filled with pizza boxes or McDonald's wrappers were usually left in his wake. It drove the more traditional chiefs wild. To add to their disdain, he'd advanced up the ranks like a bolt of lightning. He was promoted to District Chief with only eleven years on the job. That's fast in anyone's book. His personality and demeanor just didn't allow him to fall into lock step with his contemporaries. Adding insult to injury, he was an extremely intelligent and articulate man, a brilliant conversationalist. As the adage goes, he'd forgotten more about some things than any of us would ever know.

Legend has it that once, while assigned to the old SS car on Dudley Street, the chief had a short errand to do and assuming his absence wouldn't be noticed, jokingly told his aide to take command if anything happened. So what happened?

Yup, you guessed it.

Fire Alarm sent the companies to a fire in a vacant building down the street. They rolled out the doors, arrived at the location and went right to work. They raised the aerial ladder and ran a line inside. As fires go, it wasn't a big deal. Ever willing and able to do what the chief told him to do, the aide drove the chief's car to the location, put on sunglasses, the chief's white coat and helmet, and assumed a very chiefly command position in front of the building.

To honor the tradition, he conducted himself like most of the chiefs in the area.

He didn't attempt to give any orders because, for one thing, everyone was laughing like hell because they knew who he was and for another, these guys didn't need any orders to do what they did best - put the fire out.

The chief eventually returned and to show how much he cared, when apprised of the goings on, he replied, "Fire's out, right?"

We Get By With a Little Help From Our Friends

When it happens, it isn't funny. Not even a little bit. But afterwards, when the fire is out and we go back to the fire house, we have to laugh out loud at the utter stupidity exhibited by some people who, in different circumstances, might be pretty aware. And pretty smart, too. But something weird happens to people when they see a fire, especially one in their own house. Instead of getting out of the building like they're taught to do, and calling us, a lot of them figure they can do our job.

Well, they can't. Nope.

Case in point 1:

The crew of Ladder 7 rolled up to a building close to their fire house. They were the first to arrive and with Engine 17 briefly out of service at the shop getting an inspection sticker, they wouldn't have a whole lot of water until Engine 21 arrived from their quarters on Columbia Road, over a mile away.

"It's okay," the civilian said as he stood on the sidewalk at the bottom of a long flight of stairs leading up to his house, "it's only a small fire so I opened all the doors and windows for you."

The Lieutenant shook his head as he climbed down from the front seat of Ladder 7 and watched the huge column of pitch black smoke climbing skyward from behind the house. "Not a good idea," he replied as he raised his thumb like he was hitchhiking and aimed it the house.

The civilian turned around and looked behind him.

And screamed.

Case in point 2:

Outwardly unconcerned, he strolled into the firehouse. He was more than halfway to being totally inebriated. He approached the man on patrol and asked, almost haphazardly, "Ya'll got a … got a … one of them water squirting machines? Can I borrow it?"

The man on patrol replied, "Huh? A what?"

"One of them water squirting machines. The kind ya'll use."

"Fire extinguisher?"

"One of them silver suckers with the hose on it."

"That's a fire extinguisher. You want to borrow it?"

"Yeah but I swear to God, I'll bring it right back. I …. I only need it for a minute."

"Why do you want to borrow it? You have a fire?"

"Well, I was down at the Rainbow on Blue Hill. I need it for a minute. I swear to God I'll bring it back."

"Sir, why do you need it? Do you have a fire?"

"Well, yeah but it ain't a big fire."

"Where is the fire?"

"Oh, it ain't no big thing. I had this little fire in my mattress but just before I went to the Rainbow ….."

"You had a fire in your mattress?"

"Yup. But a couple of hours ago, just before I went to the Rainbow, I put the mattress in the closet. That's why I need that little silver water squirting machine."

Oh.

Case in Point 3

The first due companies rolled up to a four-story brick tenement; there was smoke rolling out the front door. The gang sprung into action - run a quick inch-and-one-half line and charge it immediately, aerial ladder to the roof, Halligan man with the engine company in case there was a door he needed to force open, sirens in the distance as the remainder of the first alarm assignment drew closer. The engine guys get into the common hallway and move forward - this should be easy, they think. The smoke is coming out the open door of the first apartment on the right. They crouch-walk into the apartment and what do they see?

A large pile of wood, on the living room floor, burning.

So, boom, boom, a few quick dashes and the fire is knocked down.

The smoke banks down of course and the laddermen start pulling the pile apart. The second due truck is here, ready to help.

The engine guys stand their ground and hit the pile with a little more water every ten seconds or so.

You seen this before, right?

Of course you have.

It's routine stuff.

But I'll be you haven't seen this part …

Suddenly, a man leaps to his feet and starts calling the firemen every kind of son-of-a-bitch you can imagine. "What the fuck are you doing?" he screams. "Get the fuck out of my house!"

One of the officers confronted the man immediately.

"Get this idiot the hell out of here," he said to no one in particular.

Two firemen take firm hold of the guy and escort him out the door and into the street. "We need a cop," one says to the chief.

The chief turns, sees a cop and motions him over.

The two firemen tell the cop what happened; the latter detains the troublemaker.

Back inside, everything is wrapping up.

Outside, the chief is satisfied that two companies will be enough to complete the job so he dismisses the extra companies.

The chief moseys over to where the cops have the troublemaker surrounded.

"What the hell is going on?" he asks.

"Those goddamned firemen fucked everything up. I was freezin' my ass off. I needed heat, man, 'cause I ain't got any."

Curious, the chief looks at the man.

"Are you telling me that you set that fire on purpose?"

"What the fuck was I s'posed to do? The landlord won't fix the furnace and I was freezin' my ass off. So fuck him. I ripped all the woodwork down with a crow bar and piled it on the floor. Then I lit it up. It was only a small fire. But like I said, I was freezin'"

CASE IN POINT 4

There was an old-time Lieutenant, WWII guy, who used to carry a bar of soap in his dungaree jacket pocket. No one knew it was there, of course, but he knew it may come in handy one day. Well, he was right.

An engine and truck were sent to a nearby apartment building to investigate an odor of gas. They were met outside by the tenant who'd made the call. Now this was long before companies carried gas meters and the like.

"There's a man working on the gas meter down the cellar," the woman said.

"Who's the guy? I don't see a gas company truck."

"He lives here. He's a weirdo."

Understanding the potential for disaster, the old-time LT told his crew to calmly evacuate the building, and then hustled into the cellar.

He couldn't believe his eyes.

The weirdo guy had disconnected the gas pipe from the service side of the meter and with the gas flowing now freely into the cellar, was busily attempting to reconnect it to a series of flexible pipes. He wanted free gas in his apartment, you see. The first section of flexible pipe was hanging down about two feet.

"Stop! Don't move!" the LT yelled.

The weirdo was startled and, amazingly, did as he was told.

The old-time LT reached into his pocket, removed the bar of soap, walked gingerly to weirdo's side and jammed it on the end of the gas line.

Just like that, the gas flow stopped.

Hey, you never know what those old-timers had up their sleeve - or in their pocket.

The Original WWF

It's about 0200.

The stillness was shattered by the inside telephone.

The man on patrol answered, listened carefully, scribbled on the chalkboard, put the receiver down, flipped the house lights on, and banged down on the house gong button.

Clang, clang, clang!

We climbed aboard our spare fire engine, a 1947 Mack pump. Our regular fire engine was in the shop for repairs and we'd gone back in time to claim a replacement. It's a testament to Mack, though; 23 years after they were delivered to the fire department, these old pumps still worked and well.

The crew tonight was one man short, although it was the typical manning level. We had an officer and only three firemen. Bobby Graham drove. I was on the back step with another jake. The boss was a fairly new Captain, a wonderful man, a real nice guy but in no way was he cut out for duty in the area we worked in. He'd spent the first few years of his fire service career in a neighboring town, and, when he finally made it to Boston, even after he made Lieutenant, he was assigned to much slower fire companies. He had over thirty years on the job by the time he made Captain and arrived at Engine 24. We all loved the old guy but, well, he was in over his head. Just a bit.

So, as we rolled down Quincy Street, there wasn't any doubt. We could see the flames above the buildings between us and where we were going.

A couple of quick turns - left on Dacia to a right on Wayland to a left on Balfour - and there we were.

All alone.

Right in front of a six family duplex going to beat the band.

Right beside a hydrant.

The Captain, in a very nervous voice, screamed into the transmitter: "Engine 24! Engine 24! We have a . . . we have a . . . a fire . . . we have a fire here!"

Bobby Graham told us later that it was funny as hell because it sounded like he didn't believe what he as seeing.

In the meantime, while I started to pull a big line out of the rear bed, the other guy on the back step with me - the hydrant man - jumped off the piece and ran into the vacant lot beside the building, screaming and waving his arms.

As they say in today's jargon, I thought, WTF?

The Captain stood still, almost mesmerized by the burning spectacle before him, the aforementioned six family duplex. I was watching him, hoping for some

Busy as Hell

kind of order about where he wanted me to go with the line. Nothing.

Then, suddenly, out of the corner of his eye, he caught sight of the disappearing fireman.

"Hey!" he yelled. "Where the hell are you going?!"

No reply from the fleeing fireman. Just more yelling and screaming and running around in little circles waving his arms.

Then, just as the fireman almost disappeared into the tall grass, the most amazing thing happened.

The Captain took off after him!

He caught up to him and tackled him!

They wrestled on the ground!

They yelled and screamed at one another!

They got up.

Then they started wrestling all over again.

Rolling over and over like two little kids in a pile of autumn leaves.

Bobby got the pump going while I dragged the line into the yard. We broke the line at 150-feet and left it laying on the ground while he and I raced to connect the pump to the hydrant. In good time, we were ready. The line was charged. The old Mack was humming. But the Captain and the other guy were still wrestling in the weeds.

We could hear the sirens of the approaching companies.

What to do, what to do?

"Bobby, help me!"

What to do, what to do?

In a heartbeat, Bobby Graham - no helmet, no jacket - was right there and together we humped the line toward the front door, about 25 feet away. Moving a charged big line with only two guys is not an easy job. It sure would have been nice if the two wrestlers had declared a draw and helped. Of course, they did eventually and both of them were covered in dried out leaves and other assorted vegetation. They looked like two camouflaged snipers.

Later on, after things settled down and we got to the business at hand, I overheard the chief as he talked with an officer from one of the companies. He said he'd reported a working fire from a half-mile away because he didn't want the Captain whacking five alarms before he got there. Oh, if the chief only knew that talking about the fire over the radio was the farthest things from that Captain's mind.

SATIN DOLL

Anyone who has ever dealt with fire buffs and sparks knows that not all of them are, well, let's say they're not always sincere or forthcoming about themselves. In an effort to be accepted, they're likely to embellish a bit to make themselves sound more palpable to the group who's acceptance they cherish. One such lad used to visit us in Grove Hall. He was nice enough, very willing to help out, and, in general, accepted for what he was - an over the road truck driver who told stories about his formative years growing up near New York City. At times he seemed to try too hard to fit in, regaling us with tall tales about his singing ability and how he used to appear with Mercer Ellington, Duke Ellington's son. In fact, none of us gave a damn. But, there were one or two guys who were determined to smoke him out.

Their day arrived when, in an amazing stroke of luck, luck like you read about, the very same Mercer Ellington was appearing in Prince Hall, the building directly next door to the firehouse. The plotters could hardly wait for our young fire buff to arrive because they knew what would happen. They would confront him with the cold hard facts, and he'd be forced to surrender and admit that he'd been lying through his teeth. What could be simpler? So, by the time the young man arrived, everyone in the fire house knew what was going to happen.

Around six o'clock, give or take, he walked in the back door and went directly into the kitchen. He said hello to everyone and engaged in small talk, probably about his most recent trip to North Carolina and where, of course, he'd buy cheap cartons of cigarettes for the smokers. Finally, one of the plotters laid the bait.

"Who was that famous guy you used to sing with in New York?"

"Mercer Ellington, Duke Ellington's son."

"You sure about that?"

"What do you mean? Of course, I'm sure," he grinned, oblivious to the trap almost sprung.

"No, really, you're sure. Positive. I mean, it wasn't some guy making believe he was this Ellington guy. He was the real deal, right?"

The smile disappeared. "What's this about? Why are you asking me these questions?"

"Well, mister big New York singer, maybe you'd like to go next door to Prince Hall and see him, see this Mercer Ellington guy. He's playing there tonight. The show starts at eight."

The young lad's face went ashen white. "Are you serious?"

"Yup, we are. Maybe it's time you admit to being a lying bastard."

The lad got up from the table and vanished through the kitchen door. No one followed him or cared where he went. The plotters had hit their mark square between the eyes.

Well almost.

The young Lad returned in about thirty minutes. Needless to say, there were a few surprised firemen still in the kitchen, a plotter among them. He asked, "Okay, you ready to admit you're full of shit?"

The young lad smiled. "No. In fact, I spoke with Mercer and he's letting me sing with the band tonight. I go on at nine o'clock. So, unless you guys have a fire, you can come over and listen to me sing Satin Doll."

What started out as a regular, old fashioned gotcha moment had turned into a (caps lock on) GOTCHA moment.

The kid sang his song and the apologies flowed.

Freely.

Sparks and various other names (some not so nice)

Of all the groups of people associated with, or at least aligned with the BFD, fire buffs (called "sparks" in Boston) are most easily pigeonholed.

According to "Pictorial History of Firefighting" by Robert W. Masters, revised edition published in 1967 by Castle Books:

"(Fire) Buffing knows no social or class distinction. Doctors, lawyers, bakers, factory workers, grocery clerks and Wall Street financiers all answer the call of bell or siren. George Washington not only chased a goodly number of fires in his day, but also donated a hand-drawn hose cart to the volunteer department of Mount Vernon. Benjamin Franklin was a familiar figure in early Philadelphia firefighting. Supreme Court Justice Oliver Wendell Holmes is remembered as a buff in Boston and Mayor Fiorello H. LaGuardia in New York City. Not to be outdone, the female 'engine chasers' are represented by no less than Mrs. [Harry] Truman."

To add to the above list of famous fire buffs, let me tell you about the cold, rainy night I was standing outside a burning building in the South End, operating

Busy as Hell

Engine 24's spare Mack pump, probably of 1947 vintage. Anyway, I'm hopping back and forth from foot to foot, trying to keep warm while watching the fire when, suddenly, a somewhat short, white haired old man appeared beside me. I looked at him and after an obvious double take, realized who it was.

"What brings you out on a cold, nasty night like this?" I asked Arthur Fiedler.

He never missed a beat - pun intended - and replied with an impish smile, "The fire, my boy. The fire."

I'd always heard that Mr. Fiedler was a big fire buff but only saw him that one time. Over the years, he'd been photographed with many different chiefs and other high ranking officers but, so far as I knew, never in a solitary situation like this one. So I felt pretty good sharing a cold, rainy couple of square yards of asphalt on Washington Street with a well-known celebrity, alone, in the middle of the night, just watching a fire together in silence. It was pretty cool.

Of course, not all fire buffs are celebrities though some have been elevated to pseudo celebrity status within their own cadre of like minded folks. They lead groups or clubs that focus their efforts in different areas of interest and there are experts in almost every facet of the fire fighting profession.

For instance, there are sparks who know more about Boston's fire engines than any one hundred jakes combined. With a glance - even at an old black and white photograph - they can tell you the make, model and year of most any fire engine and over the years, which fire companies have used it. There are sparks who can tell you which engine companies arrived at which fire alarm fire in, say, 1955 and in what order they did so. Then they top it off by listing the chiefs who were in command.

And speaking of pictures, between them all, they surely have hundreds of thousands of pictures of thousands of fires! They have pictures of everything. Pictures of burning buildings, of fire fighting operations in progress, of fire engines at fires and in quarters, candid pictures of familiar faces . . . and the list goes on. If you can think of a picture that has anything at all to do with the Boston Fire Department, chances are the picture has already been taken and has found its way into the collection of at least a dozen different sparks.

There are several kinds of sparks.

First are those - and you'd be surprised how many are women - who never became fireman. Instead, they prefer to sit on the sidelines and cheer the firemen on, much like you'd do at a football game. And there's nothing wrong with this. For them, it's just a hobby. They chase fire engines for the thrill of it all. Is it exciting? Yes, of course it is. The red lights, the sirens, the action; it's all part of the attraction and mystique. You can properly call them "harmless sparks" because they never get in the way or cause any trouble. They just show up, watch the fire, and then go home but because their hobby seems a bit out of the mainstream, these are the sparks firemen understand least of all. Why, they'll wonder, would someone leave the comfort of their home in the middle of the night and drive 10 miles to watch someone else work? Why do these people brave snowstorms and below freezing weather just to watch a building burn down? Alas, the answers aren't always easily explained. Perhaps they know a fireman. Maybe they're related to one or two. Perhaps - and I know this is true - they'd rather drive across the city to watch a building burn down than walk across the street to see the Celtics play. Some of them visit fire houses on a semi-regular basis because they've developed friendships with certain firemen over the years. No harm, no foul.

Secondly, there are those who see the department through a different set of eyes. They are interested in fires yes, but they're equally (or more) interested in the historical side of the department. They will go to fires and watch but there aren't any wannabes among them. Most are very satisfied with their chosen careers. Of course, it may seem odd to a nonchalant observer that people who have absolutely no official connection with the fire department may also be the ones with the most obvious, and therefore helpful, interest preserving historical records and documents.

We are indeed fortunate to have people like these in Boston because the facts are, and this is a sadly verifiable truth, in past years the Boston Fire Department had precious little interest in preserving its own history. There are stories of the wholesale purging of old documents to make room on shelves for newer documents of the same ilk. Sometime in 1970, or so, an entire library of old fire reports from the 1930s, 40s and 50s was summarily tossed into the nearest dumpster because they were "taking up too much room." Just thinking about the documents that found their way to the dump makes me cringe. For instance, what historian wouldn't love to have the opportunity to review the fire reports of every company that went to the fire in the Cocoanut Grove in 1942? Or the Sleeper Street fire in 1948? Or Trumbull Street in 1964? The Rutherford Avenue conflagration in 1941? Bellflower Street in 1964? Or any fire?

Perhaps, had a spark been consulted or notified, that person may have happily removed the papers and stored them in boxes in his cellar, or somewhere safe. Instead, because sparks were viewed by many as just a bunch of nuts, nothing of this sort was even thought about or considered. It's too bad because so much was lost. I mean, okay, maybe there comes a time when you have to get rid of the actual documents - the paper itself - but it wasn't as if microfilm hadn't been invented.

In a display of equally egregious lack of regard for the department's history, old black and white portrait-type photographs of deceased members were mailed to family members when older, retired members passed away. The photos were pocket-sized and they served as the official photograph of said member. When they were mailed away, they were gone for good. And it wasn't as though the families had asked for the photos, either. When a death was reported, the public relations office just went to the archives, removed the photograph and mailed it away. Poof, just like that! There's no telling how many were lost because of the ill-considered practice. Something could - should! - have been done to preserve the fire department's history. The Boston Fire Department may be run by its commanders but the history of the department belongs to everyone. While their authority to discard old items remains unchallenged, it's the lack of wisdom in ever doing so that is questioned. So we are left to congratulate those who recognized the inherent value of (and saved some of) the BFD's history while laying blame for its loss at the door of any one of the institutional hierarchies for its utter failure in this regard.

There is a third group and frankly, it is probably the most misunderstood of all the groups. It's the sparky firemen, the ones for whom chasing fire engines wasn't enough. Never content to just stand around and watch, these guys wanted to go to fires in an official capacity, on a fire engine, and they wanted to go to as many fires as possible.

These sparky firemen sit 180-degrees opposite of non-sparky firemen, the men who in many cases took a few different civil service exams after WWII (and later) and then accepted the first job offer that came along. They came to work, did their job, and went home, all the while never seeking to go to any fires beyond the ones the system tells the to go to and maybe even hoping they'll miss as many fires as possible by being at a lesser incident - like a rubbish fire - when a larger fire is reported. As you may imagine, there can be disagreements between the two when they work together.

The most obvious difference is that the non-sparky firemen, in most cases, had no idea about fire fighting. They didn't come from a fire-fighting family, didn't follow in their father's or grandfather's footsteps. So they didn't know where the firehouses were located; didn't know who was busy and who wasn't. To them, it didn't matter which engine or ladder company they were assigned to when they got the job.

On the other hand, it's pretty safe to assume that a large percentage of sparky firemen did follow the family footsteps. They were brought up listening to fire stories at the dinner table. They visited firehouses when they were little kids and met scores of old-time firemen, many of whom had advanced up the ranks to lieutenant, captain and beyond by the time they were ready to join the ranks. Unlike their non-sparky counterparts, fire fighting was in their blood.

I know because I was one of them.

After joining the BFD ranks in 1969, it was fun learning from other sparky firemen about how to best achieve our collective goals - get to as many fires as possible. Like make friends with the guys who work in the Fire Alarm Office, hoping that you'll receive preferential consideration when a special need arises.

You can imagine the uproar when we got caught sending pizzas to fire alarm one night hoping, naturally, for some extra consideration should they find themselves short an engine company. The covering Lieutenant - who was going to be here for three or four tours - found out and went right out of his mind! I can still hear him screaming that we were crazy and then, and then . . . well, he found out that three or four pizzas would keep us in fire alarm's good graces for a week or so! (I am happy to note that the ploy worked.)

Sparky firemen weren't satisfied just to go the fires they're scheduled to go to, they want to go to all the fires, all the time and it doesn't matter where the fire is. Non-sparky firemen frowned on any attempt to "change destiny," as one of them put it.

There's a sub-group of sparky firemen...the guys from out of town who gravitated to Boston and regularly rode with certain companies when certain officers were working. They'd arrive alone or in very small groups, almost never more than three. Most were from departments that didn't have near as many fires as we did. Some came more than once and in a few isolated cases, some made the trip to Boston so often that could almost pass for real Boston jakes.

One of the better known sparks was a man named Joe Farren, a native Bostonian and fire buff who had moved to Brooklyn with his family when he was a child. He soon became friendly with some New York firemen from Ladder 108, the self-proclaimed "Pride of Williamsburg." History verifies that at some point in the later 1950s, a member of Ladder 108 had to bring a child to one of Boston's hospitals for special medical treatments. Word of the New York fireman's plight reached Lieutenant Vin Bolger of Boston's Ladder 4 - who had met the members of Ladder 108 at an annual communion breakfast in New York - and he immediately made the offer of free room and board (in the firehouse), and rides back and forth to the hospital, while the Ladder 108 member was in Boston taking care of his child. Joe Farren had attended several communion breakfasts with members of both Boston and New York fire departments. When the Boston guys found out that Joe was a native Bostonian, they invited him to visit Ladder 4. And so for many years thereafter, once every year, he did - always for a week at a time. However, in the legion of sparks, one man stands head and shoulders above all the others. Now some may argue that one Mr. Ben Ellis was Spark #1. Yes, Ol' Ben was around for a long, long time and certainly went to thousands of fires during his years. But he was, first and foremost, a wealthy businessman in charge of Ellis Fire Appliance; his company sold fire related items to everyone. With all due respect and admiration for Mr. Ellis, the title of Spark #1 belongs to:

ELLIOT MALCOLM BELIN

While most of us depend on two names to properly identify ourselves, some people are well known by just one name: Jesus, Elvis, Madonna, Cher, Moe, Larry, Curly, Twiggy….Elliot.

Yup, I consider Elliot a member of this esteemed group, although for markedly different reasons than any of the above, most obviously The Three Stooges.

He has been chasing fire engines in Boston since 1942 (he was seven years old) and has the records to prove it. In fact, hundreds and hundreds of times over the period of years covered herein, 1963-1983, he supplied accurate, detailed information to fire ground commanders he knew as friends, insurance companies, news media, and to the Boston Fire Department as a whole. In fact, all the detailed information I included in the Introduction came directly from Elliot.

Despite his willingness and ability to help in any way possible, it wasn't always peaches and cream for Mr. Belin. In fact, over the years, he has most assuredly endured more ridicule from Boston firemen than any man alive. He has been bombarded with rubble from the higher floors of burned out buildings, he has been soaked more times than a Bernie Madoff client, and he has been on the receiving end of verbal abuse, the likes of which are usually reserved for the enemies of state. And why, you ask? Because very few took the time to find out what made him tick. Instead, almost everyone saw a nut job with glasses who wore a helmet and fire coat but wasn't a real live fireman and most of all, went to fires without being paid! He walked around, taking notes. Not because he was spying on us but because he was (and remains) a meticulous keeper of meticulous records.

However, there was a side to Elliot that few fireman understood - he had befriended many chief officers over the years, chiefs who had come to depend on his ability to capture information that they didn't have the time to capture on their own - because they were too busy trying to put the fire out to keep track of exactly which company ran how much hose to what floor in what building. It can be said then that Elliot made himself an indispensable feature inside the fire ground commander's overall duties. And he did his job well, very well if you believe the chiefs he helped.

Over his many years, some members ran afoul of his chief-level connections and paid the price. For example, there was a captain of a reasonably busy engine company who for some reason, absolutely hated Elliot. He'd spent sufficient time at various fires over the years aiming hose streams at him from inside buildings and generally making his life as miserable as possible. However, one evening, the captain was fed his just deserts when as acting district chief, he rushed to complain to an acting deputy chief about Elliot's presence on the fire ground. He was standing in the street, angrily pointing to Elliot, undoubtedly demanding his immediate removal from the scene.

The acting deputy listened carefully then did a most amazing thing: he summoned Elliot to the chief's meeting and asked him, "Elliot, where did you tell me you wanted the acting district chief to run the line from his regular company?"

Game, set, match

Any ideas which captain never bothered ol' Elliot again?

Using any sensible standard of measure, he's almost assuredly been to more fires in Boston than anyone in history. Where regular members only responded when they were working, Elliot went to every working fire, multiple alarm fire, one-alarm fire, and fires lost to history. There was a time in 1968 - there were more than 800 fires such in the city - when his calculations reveal that he was either going to, or coming home from a fire every 12 hours.

His ability to keep and maintain impeccable records was only part of the story. Everyone would agree that almost without exception, fire ground commanders don't want civilians in the way while they're trying to do their job. However, Elliot's presence at every fire helped convince many fire ground commanders that he could be depended upon to help out in a pinch. At one such multiple alarm fire, the deputy chief saw Elliot standing nearby and asked him if he'd locate a portable generator then find two firemen, pump operators, maybe, and ask them to help him carry it to the front of the building. Elliot obliged then turned and left to find the generator. Locating one, he looked around and saw two men standing a short distance away. He explained the deputy's order to the firemen and asked them to help him carry the appliance. But he wasn't finished, no sir. So imagine the deputy's surprise when Elliot returned with the generator, two firemen and two helpers ... a mailman and a Hood milkman.

Of Elliot Belin, let it be said once and for all - he is the ultimate Boston spark. And if the city could figure a way to charge admission to watch its fires, they would. Yet, something tells me that they'd give Elliot a season ticket - a free one.

...Bob

I have a friend.

His name is Bob. We went to high school together. We were appointed to the fire department together. Our paths crossed many times over the years; a fire here, a fire there. Yet, somewhere along the line we lost touch. Eventually, he retired early and moved out of state. We remained in intermittent email contact, our decades old friendship was pretty much a thing of the past. So when we he told me recently that he would be back in Massachusetts for a visit, I jumped at the opportunity to meet with him again. There was the usual reason - to renew an old friendship - but there was another reason; I wanted to interview him for Busy As Hell and either dispel of verify the rumors I'd heard about him.

You see, Bob's career was - and I quote Winston Churchill - "A riddle wrapped in a mystery inside a dilemma." There was not then, nor is there now, any defendable rhyme or reason for the way he was treated by some of the BFD's self-professed big shots or by some of the rank and file members he met on his journey from fire fighter to Fire Lieutenant to Fire Captain and finally, to District Fire Chief.

Those who knew him best understood his soft personal manner and lack of interest in crossing swords with anyone. In short, for reasons only he understood, Bob seldom responded to the attacks upon his good name or his equally good character. He chose to ignore the idiots who maligned his very presence and instead, set out to be the best fireman he could be. The rationale was obvious, and simple: defeat the detractors by outthinking them or, if that wasn't enough, by outranking them.

Now, there is little doubt but that Bob is one of the single most professionally motivated fire chiefs the BFD ever produced. His dedication to his craft may be matched, but it's never been surpassed and likely never will. It is also very questionable whether any chief in the history of the Boston Fire Department has had as many topical articles published in fire service trade publications during their career - at last count it is more than 120. However, as you may have already figured out - surely, the Star of David at the top of the chapter is a tip off - Bob had a problem. He was born a Jew, or, as he was often called by some, "that fuckin' Jew."

I have no plans to launch into a long, drawn out discussion about Jews and Israel. However, even the most skeptical observer would have to admit that the Jewish race has no shortage of people who hate them for no other reason than, well, their Jewishness. It's a generational thing, I guess. It's a prejudice passed along through the ages. It's not about Judaism itself, the actual religion. It has nothing to do with what goes on inside a temple or synagogue, principally because there aren't a hundred non-Jews in Boston who can tell you the first thing about what transpires when Jews gather to worship. No, it's something deeper than that. It's a vile and hateful prejudice that has spawned a thousand myths about Jews and Judaism. You've heard some of them, I assume: Jews run this, Jews run that, Jews have all the money, Jews own this industry, etc. Knowing what we know about such things, it's easy to see that Bob had two strikes against him the day he was sworn in and became a Boston fireman.

But what of his devotion to the job, to his fellow firefighters?

What about his interest in making things better and safer for the rank and file?

Let me give you a for instance . . . years ago, a major manufacturer brought a new fireman's "wheat light" to the marketplace. It was a handy gadget that attached to the front of the fire coat, just over the left breast. It was wildly successful, and in short order every Boston Jake had one, as did tens of thousands of other Firefighters across the USA.

But what the company doesn't tell you - and they're not obligated to - is that they developed their light after visiting Boston and meeting with the fireman who had the idea in the first place – our friend, Bob. Yes, it took the manufacturer three years to develop it, test it, and bring it to market. And, yes, they were under no obligation to tell anyone what they were doing, but here's where it gets dicey.

During the product development stage, this manufacturer apparently called the Boston Fire Department and spoke to a civilian employee of the department who had been present when Bob made his presentation of the light he had developed. During the call, they asked the civilian whether Bob had anything to do with the development of the light. The civilian employee said that Bob did not. In other words, he lied through his teeth.

But why?

When the new light was finally unveiled, Bob called the company and asked what was going on. They politely told him that while he had neglected to file for a patent, they had not. There was nothing Bob could do but kick himself in the ass for being so trusting and naive as to have any faith in those he'd met three years previous. I suppose this confounded his detractors. What kind of Jew was he? Couldn't even file for a patent and protect his ass. How many millions of dollars did he screw himself out of by trusting that people would tell the truth about his proprietary concept? Stupid Jew.

Bob was also out of the mainstream because his interest in the fire service transcended the issues found in Boston. Over the years, he developed what became a lifelong interest in the problems associated with wildfires. Granted, it's not a subject that city departments pay a lot of attention to so you can likely imagine how his suggestions on the matter were received . . . that's right, not well at all. Undaunted, and for years, he hounded the brain trust with his belief that they should consider having a brush truck or two in case there was, well, a large brush fire in the city limits. But the brain trust balked. Why would the city of Boston need a brush fire truck? The regular pumps had hose and water, didn't they? They'd suffice, wouldn't they?

Of course, the powers that be, in rejecting Bob's ideas, refused to consult their own history, a history replete with issues that needed to be addressed during what is often called "grass fire season." The areas that were annually most affected lie in the southern most portions of the city: West Roxbury and Hyde Park. There are (or were) eight companies that covered the area - Engines 30, 45, 48, 53, 55 and Ladders 16, 25, 28 and, for a short time (from 1975-1981), Ladder 5. Yet, during grass fire season, additional engine companies would routinely be relocated for the tour of duty to help pick up the slack.

Then one windy day, a brush fire on Enneking Parkway in Hyde Park got out of hand. The fire raced across the ground then suddenly exploded into the trees. I was there. I saw it. It consumed tree tops and set off towards a line of homes. We were ordered to withdraw from the woods and relocate to a position near the threatened homes. In short order, three alarms had been ordered. Lines of hose were run into the woods; some were filled with water. One of the more enduring memories I have is one of a lone firefighter standing in the back yard of a home, a nozzle in his hand. The hose attached to the nozzle is only three feet long. It had burned through as it laid on the ground waiting to be filled with water. The wildfire was eventually extinguished but not before several eyes were opened to the issues Bob had been talking about for years. Bob was home at the time of the fire and saw the news reports on television that evening. As he left for work the following day, he knew his phone would ring.

He was right.

On the other end of the call was the BFD's second in command, the Chief of Operations - his message was clear. Bob was asked to bring a complete report to fire headquarters on wildfire operations and, also, a list of exactly what the department needed to beg, borrow, steal, jury-rig, or purchase in order to have two brush trucks pressed into service forthwith. In typical fashion, Bob had anticipated this request. He showed up, loaded for bear. In short order, two older fire engines were re-fitted and pressed into service.

Additional examination of his career will reveal a series of definitive successes that were ignored for no balanced, grounded reason except to conceal an extreme professional jealousy. One such incident stands out - the so-called Yellowstone fires of 1988. That's right, Yellowstone National Park in Wyoming. You see, Bob was (and remains) a nationally known and well-respected Structure Protection Specialist. He knows his business, but there's a problem. Wildfire tactics and strategy is as common in Boston as, say, blizzards in Honolulu. No one knows much about wildfires and, frankly, no one cares. So, while fires raged in Yellowstone Park, no one in Boston was affected and so didn't worry about it.

But the federal government cared. They consulted their data base of experts and sought to bring as much talent to bear on the problem as possible. They reached out to certified wild-land firefighters all over the country. If you could help them, they wanted you in Wyoming. So, of course, Bob got the call. When he asked his immediate supervisor, a deputy chief, for permission to accept the federal entreaty, his request was denied. Puzzled, he waited until the federal government asked him a second time before again asking for permission to accept.

Request denied.

Again.

Why?

Bob's career was filled with whys.

Questions remain unanswered to this day.

Why was a notification he posted on a fire house bulletin board defaced with a swastika?

Why, when he answered a phone call on a public pay phone inside the fire house, after giving a televised PR piece about the BFD on a Boston TV channel and was greeted with "Get off the job, you stink fuckin' Jew. We don't need any fuckin' Jews on our job."

Why was he purposely railroaded by a hateful officer and "Shanghaied" to a remote fire company as punishment for an accident he hadn't caused? This same officer regularly referred to him as "that lousy fuckin' Jew."

Why did he have a tool thrown at him from a second floor window as he stood in front of a fire building?

Why was he was ignored and ostracized?

Over his thirty-two years, Bob endured more abuse than anyone. At what point should any sensible person expect the anti-Semitism to stop? Why did it continue unabated for all those years? And for what, because he's a Jew?

Well, here's a news flash . . .

Beginning in about 1966 - three years before he was appointed to the Boston Fire Department - Bob attended the Ruggles Street Baptist Church in Boston and became a follower of Jesus Christ.

In other words, for every single minute of his thirty-two year Boston Fire Department career, Bob was a Christian.

For all the grief and misery, for all the hatred that came his way, he did what Jesus would have done …. Bob turned the other cheek and showed himself to be the better man.

God bless him.

"X" Marks The Spot

It was a seasonably cold winter night with a light snow falling. There was an inch or so already on the ground.

The two lieutenants, one from the engine and the other from the truck, were standing near the front door talking about nothing in particular and watching the traffic go by. They perked up a bit when they heard the inside phone ring.

After listening, the man on house watch yelled over the loud speaker, "Both companies. Jumper in the window - on West Newton Street. No number."

The lieutenants scurried to their respective fire engines, and when crews were aboard, the apparatus raced out the doors turned right and headed for West Newton Street.

When they turned off of Tremont Street on to West Newton, there was a small crowd gathered on the right side of the street. Everyone was looking up, some were pointing to the man sitting on the third floor windowsill, his legs dangling outside.

The crews walked over to the building, and the engine Lieutenant turned to the ladder Lieutenant, asking, "What's the plan? You're the ones with the life net."

The ladder lieutenant took a quick look around at the gathered crowd then looked up to the jumper. Then he whistled. When the jumper looked, the ladder lieutenant raised his finger in the air as if to say "Wait a minute" then went over to the nearest parked automobile. With some effort, and while still looking at the jumper, he reached over and onto the roof and dragged his hand diagonally across from corner to corner. Then he shifted a bit and repeated the move, only this time he dragged his hand through the snow so that the second line crossed the first line, making an X in the snow.

Then the ladder lieutenant, with just the right amount of flair, looked back up at the jumper and motioned for him to go ahead and jump. "Here's your target," he yelled to the jumper. "Please try to land on the X so it'll be easier for us to pick you up and take you to the morgue."

The engine lieutenant covered his face and laughed, "Have you lost your mind?"

"Let's see if I have," came the reply as he again motioned for the jumper to jump and hit the X.

"You guys are crazy!" the jumper yelled down as he pulled his legs up, turned his butt on the windowsill, went back inside the apartment, and closed the window.

The ladder lieutenant looked at his counterpart and said, "He wasn't going to jump. If he was, he wouldn't have been sitting outside, freezing his ass off. He'd have already jumped. Now let's get the hell out of here before he changes his mind and climbs back out the window."

Arson For Free
(As opposed to arson for hire)

Yes, it's true.

A few of us, those who were assigned to Engine 24, a nifty little one-company fire house situated at 434 Warren Street, right on the corner of Quincy Street, actually worked with a fireman who set buildings on fire while he was off duty. And more than once while he was on duty!

If you asked any of us about those times - which well pre-dated the Fenway fires of the late 70s and the arson ring of the early 80s - those who worked with this unnamed individual (now deceased) would say, yes, we were very suspicious about his extracurricular activities.

From what I've been told, arson is one of the most difficult crimes to prove. You nearly have to see the perp with the match in their hand and watch them touch the match to, say, a pile of paper to obtain a conviction.

Now, I know zero about psychology so, I'll not get into any speculation about what a head-shrinker may conclude about the variety of callouses that are surely growing on the gray matter inside an arsonists brain. But I know this for certain: unless the arsonist is a for-hire professional, one who used timing devices to ignite the fire after he was far away, most people who light buildings on fire like to hang out in the crowd and watch the firefighters tackle their handiwork. This explains why arson inspectors make it a point to scan the crowd for familiar faces.

Right from the beginning, this guy on Engine 24 was different. Not different funny - different weird. Eventually, he earned the nickname The Flaming Arrow, eventually shortened to just The Arrow, and then, finally, for us, in these pages, to TFA.

More than anything else, TFA wanted to rescue someone and win a medal. Hey, a lot of firemen rescue people and win medals but very few really want to and no one, no one, goes out of their way to try. But this guy wanted one more than anything. In his mind, he doubtless saw himself standing on a stage at the Fireman's Ball, proudly, while the mayor hung some shiny hardware on his chest. But it never happened for him. The stars were never aligned.

So, his logic, such as it was, undoubtedly decided his course of action. If he wanted to reach that hallowed hall where valor, daring, and courage are honored, three things had to happen:

TFA had to save someone, anyone - no rescue, no medal.

If the fires where he could rescue someone weren't happening while he was working, he couldn't get a medal.

So, in order to get a medal, he had to make fires happen when he was working.

Makes sense, no?

So how did we know TFA was lighting fires?

Well, early on, there were two instances. The first involved an abandoned car in the vacant lot behind the fire house. One day, out of the clear blue sky, it suddenly caught fire. TFA saw it first and alerted everyone in the fire house. We drove the fire engine around back, squirted some water for a few minutes and put the fire out. No big deal. We didn't suspect him because, well, why would anyone believe that one of our own could be responsible when the neighborhood around us was filled with kids young enough and mischievous enough to do something stupid like light an abandoned car on fire? We just put the thing out and promptly forgot about it. But some time later, in what turned out to be a rare moment of candor, TFA told us he lit the car on fire. He laughed and said he wanted Engine 24 to have more runs than Engine 12 so he set the fire. He emphasized that it was only a small, little car fire - like a Ford Pinto, maybe - and that no one was hurt. Sure, we thought he was stupid, but to us, the incident didn't go much beyond prank status.

The second incident involved a vacant building right next door to the fire house. It happened on a bright, pleasant day, the kind that lets you leave the front apparatus door wide open. We were in the kitchen having coffee - we'd just finished doing our daily house cleaning chores - when a man wearing muddy boots and a hard hat walked into our quarters. We recognized him as one of the contractors working on repaving Warren Street. He told us there was a fire in the attic of the building next door. We laughed, of course, thinking he was joking. Someone said, "Yeah, right," but the man's expression told us he was serious. One of the guys took a look out through the side window. "Holy shit!" he exclaimed as he saw the smoke rolling out the attic windows of the building next door. We notified Fire Alarm of the situation, pulled the fire engine outside, donned our gear, which at the time consisted of dungaree jackets and a helmet, and ran an inch-and-a-half line into the attic. The fire wasn't much and we had it put out in a few minutes. Ladder 23 showed up and took care of tearing down the ceilings and walls.

As we dragged the hose out of the building and started to pack it back on the fire engine, the guy who reported the fire was off to the side talking to the Lieutenant, an officer from a quiet fire company in an outlying section of the city who was detailed to us for the day.

After a short while, we were back inside the fire house. Nothing was out of the ordinary, as far as we knew. Sometime later the detailed Lieutenant approached two of us who were standing outside the front door watching the traffic navigate through the construction, which was always an event.

"You know, in all my time on the job, that's the first time I ever walked to a fire," he said, with a laugh. We laughed with him and told him that we'd never walked to a fire, either.

Then the laughter faded and he seemed to grow pensive, serious. We noticed his change in demeanor and waited - he seemed to be searching for something to say.

"Everything okay, Loo," one of us asked.

"Well, I'm not sure," he replied with some hesitation in his voice.

"No, really, what's wrong?" we asked.

"Okay," he replied. "That guy with the white T-shirt, the guy who drove the pump out of quarters. Who is he?"

We gave him the name.

"I don't know how to say this," he began, "'cause I

never heard anything like this before. The construction guy told me that he saw that guy, the tall guy in the white T-shirt go into that house ten minutes before the fire. I think he lit the goddamned thing!"

So there it was.

Proof.

Our fellow fire fighter was a torch, an arsonist.

Obliquely, we confronted him. A little bit. We told him we knew what he was doing and that he better knock it off because he was going to get caught. He never admitted anything. He just grinned and walked away.

Over time and odd as it seems now, the little fire next door was something we more or less dismissed. We knew he did it, but it all seemed so childish. It was more like the car fire he started behind the fire house, only this time it was a ten-cent fire in a vacant building. To us, yeah, of course, it was illegal, but it wasn't overly dangerous or life threatening. We just did what we always did ... grab some hose, walk upstairs, squirt the water, watch the laddermen work, drag the hose back downstairs and go home. Compared to all the "real" fires we were going to, it didn't amount to a proverbial hill of beans. So, while our youthful, foolish side made light of it all, in what must have been an effort to convince ourselves that it was much ado about nothing, our other, more sensible side, concluded, beyond any doubt, that TFA was a few French fries short of a Happy Meal.

But then one warm, early summer night, everything changed.

If scorched buildings had been the stakes they played for on Poker Stars, TFA would have pushed a big pile of those little green Monopoly houses toward the center of the table and said, "I'm all in."

A little background ... the union was in negotiations with the city and any new information about the collective bargaining progress was always appreciated by the rank and fire firefighters. So, because we had an acceptable number of men for the tour, we did what almost every comparable fire company did: we sent an on-duty member to the union meeting to gather information. Well, on this particular night, the Lieutenant sent TFA.

Later, about 10:00 pm, there were three of us sitting on the cement steps at the rear of the firehouse, just talking. Our vantage point gave us a good view of Quincy Street and all the traffic coming toward us from a parallel thoroughfare, Blue Hill Avenue.

Suddenly, our ears tuned in to what was the unmistakable sound of a speeding car as it raced up Quincy Street towards the fire house. As was customary, we kind of tipped out heads toward the noise and listened for the crash, expecting the idiot driver to hit something. Instead, we saw a vehicle racing up the street and then, just as suddenly, it slowed with a screech and turned hard left into our little parking lot.

It was TFA, returning from the union meeting. And he damn near hit the chain link fence when he stopped. Then, in a flash, he threw the driver's side door open, exited his hot rod and started racing around the back of his car aiming himself toward the back door of the fire house.

At this very instant, the department phone, the "inside phone," rang with a long ring, i.e., as opposed to a regular, short ring. This is the inside scoop, this is Fire Alarm code for, "Saddle up boys, you're going somewhere."

As one of the guys ran to answer the phone, the rest of us jumped up and headed toward the apparatus. The Lieutenant was already sliding the pole. He'd heard the long ring, too.

The fireman who answered the phone yelled out, "Inside. Woodcliff near Dacia." That was all the information we needed. What kind of fire it was and where it was.

We all climbed aboard the fire engine just before TFA who, by now, in his haste to get his gear from his locker and get on the fire engine, was roughly three feet off the ground with excitement. The adrenaline rush on display would rival that of an Indy 500 driver approaching the first turn at 220 mph.

"It's a fuckin' fire! I know it's a fire!" he screamed.

At the time, we didn't pay attention to his warnings - we had already figured as much ourselves - but his antics were, in a word, hilarious. His face was beet red, his eyes looked like wheel covers from a '58 Buick, and he kept screaming, "It's a fuckin' fire! I know it is!"

Well, the fire alarm office had received enough phone calls to know that there was, indeed, a fire going on. So, they performed the next step. They transmitted the nearest box, 1761, Blue Hill Avenue and Woodcliff Street, thus guaranteeing a full first alarm assignment and, maybe, enough help to take care of business.

The diesel engine roared to life as the fire house bells came alive, punching out the signal:

• ＊＊＊＊＊＊＊ ＊＊＊＊＊＊ •

Engine 24 rolled straight out the door, made a wide arc, a partial left-hand turn across the intersection of Warren and Quincy, then reversed direction 180-degrees to starboard and raced down Quincy Street.

Then the radio came alive: "On box 1761," the Fire Alarm operator, said, "we're receiving calls for a building fire on Woodcliff Street near Dacia

Street. Car 7?"

Car seven responded, "Okay."

Yeah, he knew.

We rolled lickety-split down Quincy Street, turned left on to Blue Hill Avenue and there it was - a sky filled with orange. The flames were visible over the rooftops of the buildings between us and the fire. Woodcliff Street was a scant few hundred feet farther down and the Lieutenant, the coolest customer on the planet, knowing what lay ahead, waited until he had a clear view of the situation before he told the Fire Alarm guys what was happening.

Of course, only a minute or two had passed since TFA roared into the parking lot, but now there he was literally dancing about on the diamond plate in the jump seat and screaming. "It's a fuckin' fire!" This time, however, he had more than his word to convince us he was right. He was pointing to the orange obviousness in the sky ahead, and he was more than smiling. He was ... well, he looked possessed.

The other two of us in the jump seat - me and Kenny Rogers - started tightening our wheat light belts around our dungaree jackets. We knew what lay ahead.

As luck would have it, I was the pipe man this night and would therefore have the pleasure of dragging the hose up the front steps, through the front door and into the first floor.

Kenny was the loop man; he would throw a rope around the hydrant, jump on the back step and yell, "Go!" The rope, now secured at the hydrant and connected to the hose in the rear hose bed, would pull the hose out as the fire engine drove to the fire.

TFA was the so-called "bag man" - his job was to dress the hydrant which meant that after Kenny looped the hydrant and the pump drove to the fire, he would connect the hose from the rear hose bed to the 4 ½-inch outlet on the hydrant, giving us a water supply.

The rest is routine, everyday stuff. We turned the corner on to Woodcliff Street, the Lieutenant told Fire Alarm that we had fire showing on two floors of a vacant, three-story frame building, and then we went to work. Engine 12 and the RPU (an odd configuration of a rescue van and a pump), Ladders 4 and 23 showed up, and together we made pretty short work of the situation.

But a funny thing happened while we were still working inside the building. As you may suspect, rumors about TFA had spread quickly around the department in recent weeks and months. So when someone from another company walked over to TFA and asked him, point blank, "Hey, asshole! Did you light this fuckin' joint on fire?" we weren't really surprised.

But TFA didn't answer, directly.

He just smiled a wide-eyed and sinister looking smile, and then he made a laughing sound. The kind of sound you know for sure is roaming around somewhere inside Stephen King's brain.

It was eerie.

He didn't admit setting the fire.

But he admitted setting the fire.

In an hour or so, the fire was out. We all went back to the fire house, more well informed than before we arrived but a little quieter than usual.

This was the beginning of a worrisome time for the officers and members of Engine 24. What we'd all suspected might be true, what our reticent minds didn't want to accept as true, was now proven factual. There could be no other explanation for TFA's conduct that night. The direction he came from, the timing, the way he drove into the parking lot and exited his car, the overly animated gestures, the yelling, his assurances that we had a fire and then, the cherry on top, the incident inside the building ... it all pointed to one thing:

We were working with a serial arsonist.

Not just a stupid prankster.

He shared our fire house.

He ate with us.

We knew his wife, his kids.

He knew ours.

But this was different.

This was the wake-up call.

The light was on inside his head but no one was home.

It was one thing to suspect him of being a half-assed, prankster arsonist - and being the center of attention was something TFA never got tired of. He actually enjoyed the celebrity, but this, this! was something altogether different.

Now, we were sure.

This guy wasn't just a whacko any more.

He was dangerous.

But TFA didn't learn. He stopped lighting fires when we were working, but he didn't stop his shenanigans. In fact, there were rumors flying around for months and more than a few were, well, let's just say TFA and his hijinks provided a plausible explanation for several fires in and around the Roxbury-Dorchester area. The Arson Squad, composed of fellow firemen and a cop or two, was hot on his tail and closing in.

Then one night, in the middle of the night, while he was alone on house patrol, he suddenly turned on the house lights, set the house gong to clanging, and yelled as the crew slid the poles, "Over there! There's a fire right over there!"

He pointed out the side windows of the fire house to the fire roaring out the attic windows of the vacant house on the opposite side of Quincy Street, just down the block, 200 feet away.

One of the guys asked no one in particular, "How the hell did he manage to do that?!"

Another answered in his typical pithy, laconic style, "He used a fuckin' flaming arrow, that's how!"

So, now with his new moniker hung about his neck, TFA went on to bigger and better things. He started setting even more fires when he was off duty. And he didn't restrict his activities to Boston. He'd drive around in his car, looking for places to burn down; a vacant house here, a factory there.

He was eventually arrested of course, then tried and convicted on at least one count of arson.

So, off he went, to prison.

And, too, I might add, without a medal.

There Are Medals
(Well, Not Always)

"A soldier will fight long and hard for a bit of colored ribbon," Napoleon once said. And to that end, adding a semi-verification to the undersized French general's beliefs, precious few things spark as much conversation, interest, controversy, and/or unmitigated disdain or derision as the awarding of medals for bravery.

Although I've never known a fireman who arrived at a fire and then tried to win a medal, I'd guess it would be fairly easy to believe that there are some, maybe even a lot, who secretly wanted a medal. But in practice, it's impossible to script the events and subsequent reactions to these events that transform an otherwise ordinary situation into something deserving of recognition.

In other words, rescues and the medals they beget aren't made, they just happen. You go to a fire, you do your job, and someone decides that your efforts went above and beyond the normal call of duty. When this happens, someone "writes you up" and the process begins.

There is no hard and fast rule about how, or where,

a so-called write up begins. Some originate with the company officer. The Fire Captain or Fire Lieutenant in command of the company will write a report indicating what actions were taken by the fireman in question and then pass the report along through channels. Others are written by the District Chief in charge at the incident - probably because most rescues are solitary events and the company officer doesn't always see what took place.

All such recommendations are investigated by the Deputy Fire Chief. If the Deputy Chief approves the recommendation, he will forward it to headquarters. The department will then issue an official commendation in General Orders; the fireman will be identified, the event will be described in detail and then will be "referred to the Board of Merit for further consideration." However, if he investigates and then disapproves the recommendation, the issue is settled. No further action will be taken.

Then, once per year during each of the war years , the Board of Merit - made up of all Deputy Chiefs - meets to decide which firemen, if any, are deserving of being awarded either of three medals:

The John E. Fitzgerald Medal (Most Meritorious Act)

The Walter Scott Medal For Valor

The Patrick J. Kennedy Medal of Honor

There are three categories of risk that the Board of Merit considers when making their collective decision: Unusual, Great, and Extreme. Naturally, the greater the risk involved the better chance the fireman has to receive a medal.

If a rescue involves what the Board considers unusual personal risk, the lowest of the three categories, in almost all cases, the fireman who performed the act will have his name placed on the Roll of Merit - a rather long list of members who have distinguished themselves in a manner just below the Great or Extreme personal risk categories.

But here's the rub. Some chiefs didn't believe in medals. At all. Ever. It didn't matter what the fireman did or what the company officer recommended; some chiefs wouldn't recommend anyone for anything. It's been said that these guys wouldn't even commend their own mothers for a job well done.

On the other hand, some chiefs like medals. If they believe the effort was even approaching above and beyond the call of duty, they'll recommend without hesitation. I have had it explained to me by one such chief officer that medals are good for the department as a whole - they're publicized during the annual fireman's ball and they enhance the morale of the fire-fighting force in general. I'm not so sure I believe all of that, but it does explain this particular chief's reasoning.

There is also another divide to consider. Of those chiefs who do like medals, some can write like Hemingway while others write like Humpty Dumpty. This will often lead to comparisons of the duties performed by those who win medals and those who do not. Common comments heard in the fire house kitchens might be:

"I just can't believe that guy won a medal when Harry did something ten times better the month before."

The reply to which may be:

"Yeah, but you know him, he hates writing people up. No one on his group ever wins anything. But that other guy? He'll write you up for coming to work on time. And he can write, too."

And so on.

In other words, the entire medal process is subjective. And because it is, the conversation, interest, controversy, and/or unmitigated disdain or derision enter the picture and, in some cases, clouds the issue.

Are there firemen without medals who deserved to be decorated? Sure there are. Are there fireman who probably didn't deserve to be decorated? Probably.

And this is true mostly because of the way some

chiefs viewed the aforementioned methodology. The bottom line is that some chiefs didn't believe that a fireman doing his job deserved anything more than what he signed on for - a paycheck.

But when you step back and see it for what it is - again, a subjective process - and for all the questions and such, the Deputy Chiefs usually got it right.

But not always.

Personally, I have been involved in only one write-up.

To set the stage, about seventeen months before the incident we'll talk about, Ladder 30, the ladder company that had shared Engine 42's quarters since 1913, had been disbanded. At the time, Ladder 30 had been replaced with Rescue 2 until they, too, were disbanded.

So when Engine 42 responded alone to a reported fire at 277 Centre Street - a four-story brick apartment building and part of the Bromley Heath housing project - we did so knowing there would be no immediate ladder company support.

Upon arrival, we found fire showing from three windows on the second floor. While the pump operator nosed into a hydrant and prepared to connect the front suction, three of us - Joe Clark, Jack Brignoli (who was detailed in from Ladder 7) and yours truly - immediately ran an inch-and-a-half line into the stairwell and started up the stairs.

Knowing the first due truck, Ladder 10, had to come from farther away, I carried a Halligan bar and maul inside with us. When we arrived at the landing, we couldn't gain entrance to the apartment because the heavy, steel-clad door was locked up tighter than a drum. Joe and Jack went to work; the paint on the door was bubbling and smoke was seeping out into the hallway from around the door frame. Then, just as the inch-and-a-half line sprang to life, I heard someone scream. It came from outside, down in the courtyard. I took a quick look. There was a frantic man pointing to the windows just beyond where the fire was showing. "There's a kid in there!" he screamed. "There's a kid in there!"

Jack was standing right beside me. He heard the man, too. "I'm gonna find another way in," he said and took off down the stairs.

While Joe continued working with the Halligan bar, I called Ladder 10 on the portable and told them we needed a ladder in the courtyard - not to worry, they'd already started doing exactly that. Then, with the line laying on the floor and ready to use, I laid on the floor and tried to use my legs as a battering ram against the door. After several good, hard kicks, and with Joe applying the leverage, the door gave. Joe and I crouched down and pushed the line inside.

Now here's where things get interesting.

As we moved through the doorway, in the instant before Joe opened the nozzle, I caught a brief glimpse of Ladder 10's ground ladder - it was vertical and was just starting to fall against the building. In the next instant, I could not believe what I saw: Jack was already near the top of the ladder - he had started climbing when the ladder was still vertical - and I watched in astonishment as he hunched up his shoulders, tucked his head and face turtle-like under his helmet and inside the collar on his fire coat and then dove head first through the glass window into the apartment.

Joe and I continued to crawl and push the line farther into the apartment and started making headway, only to meet Jack face to face as he crawled out of the back bedroom and into the living room toward us. He had already found the child and passed him out the window to a fireman on Ladder 10 who had followed him up the ground ladder.

From the time Ladder 10 arrived and started to raise the ground ladder, until this point, right now, a whole sixty-seconds had passed.

In five more minutes, it was all over. We had all the help we needed; two more engine companies and another truck. Everyone would agree that the fire wasn't much as fires go - a couple of rooms in a brick apartment building - in and out, that was it.

But I still couldn't believe what I had seen. When we got back to quarters, I notified the District Chief and the Deputy Chief about the incident. They both told me to write it up. So I did. To my mind, there was no way any sensible person could have seen what Jack did and then categorize the act as having been anything less than "extreme personal risk."

Think about it:

Jack had no idea what awaited him beyond that window.

What if he'd jumped head first against a bureau?

Or against anything that could stop him?

What if the glass had sliced his throat wide open?

What if anything had happened except what happened?

He would have hurtled to the cement courtyard, two floors below.

He could have been killed.

But he just reacted.

Call it instinct, call it crazy.

What Jack Brignoli did that day was selfless.

He deserved recognition. Lots of recognition.

But all he got was the shaft.

Yes, okay, Jack Brignoli's name was placed on the Roll of Merit, no small honor. But the Board of Merit, in its wisdom, if you can call it such, awarded only two medals that year. They awarded the John E. Fitzgerald and the Walter Scott Medals. No one received the Patrick Kennedy Medal of Honor because, according to the Board of Merit, no one deserved it.

There's only two words to describe this shunning.

Pure bullshit.

And that's exactly what it was.

The District Chief who had the fire and the Acting Deputy Chief - the highly esteemed veteran fire officer, John P. Vahey - in command in the division where the fire occurred investigated the incident and came to the same conclusion that I came to when I wrote the paper: Jack Brignoli had subjected himself to extreme personal risk in saving that young lad. He had reached the upper limit of the risk analysis.

However, the proof of the intentional snub was in the written pudding.

The general orders that were published in October 1982 announcing Jack's actions read, in part:

Because Fire Fighter Brignoli acted in a manner reflecting much credit to our profession and because this life saving rescue was made before fire operations had begun, exposing himself to extreme personal risk ...

Guess what. The above words were omitted from the general order announcing Jack's name being added to the Roll of Merit in May 1983 and from the Fireman's Ball program issued that year. In their place, other words from the general orders - "without hesitation entered" - were focused upon. In the Board of Merit's collective mind, Jack's had no longer exhibited a willingness to endure extreme personal risk to save someone's life, he just acted without hesitation.

Again, pure bullshit!

These facts - the rescue, the shunning - beg the question, why?

Why was Jack knocked down a peg when it came time to recognize him for the amazing feat he had performed?

Well, the answer isn't pretty. But it's understandable.

You see, Jack was a rabble-rouser, a bomb tosser, a man who made no bones about bucking the status quo. Some would say that he took no small measure of delight in making some people uncomfortable if he saw something - almost always safety related - that he believed should be, or shouldn't be part of the department's standard operating procedure. He once made a major stink over the placement of a large metal box on the side of the ladder truck, the box that held the K12 saw. It was positioned in such a way that it partially obscured the tillerman's line of sight along the side of the ladder truck. In other words, it was a safety hazard. The box just didn't belong there. It should have been placed somewhere else. But it wasn't.

So, who paid the price for making sure it was corrected? Not the brain trust who ordered that the box be mounted there in the first place. Not a chance. Jack paid the price because to some people, the desk drivers, he was a royal pain in the ass. To others, he was a tough-as-nails supporter of the rank and file firemen who gave no quarter and expected none in return. Jack was not swayed by rank or threats, however veiled or concealed.

So, Jack was left to accept that there is a human element, a often sinister human ingredient, to the entire process of awarding medals. It's wrong, but it's the way it is.

Now let's add some insult to the injury: The two Patrick J. Kennedy Medals that were awarded the years before and the year after Jack Brignoli's actions were awarded for what was determined to be "great personal risk," one step below "extreme personal risk."

Whether they loved him, hated him, or remained indifferent, there was one thing they all agreed upon: if your ass was trapped in a fire, Jack Brignoli was the guy you'd want to come looking for you. RIP, old friend.

BUSY AS HELL

ROLL OF MERIT

is hereby awarded to
FIRE FIGHTER
JOHN T. BRIGNOLI
A Member of Ladder Co. 7

On September 14, 1982, at 0958 hours, Engine Company 42 responded to Box 2411 for an alarm of a fire at 277 Centre Street, Jamaica Plain.

Upon arrival, heavy fire and smoke were issuing from the second floor apartment whereupon several people informed them of a child trapped in the building.

Fire Lieutenant W. Michael Foley of Engine Company 42 and Fire Fighter John Brignoli of Ladder Company 7 (detailed to Engine Company 42) donned air masks and entered the building via the front stairway. Under heavy smoke conditions, both made their way to the apartment door and made several attempts to gain entrance but were unable to do so due to the heavy metal construction of the door.

Fire Fighter Brignoli then descended the stairway and ascended a ladder that was being put into position by Ladder Company 10 and without hesitation entered the smoke and heat filled room, conducted a successful search and passed the child to fire fighters on the ladder outside the room. Both Fire Fighter Brignoli and the child were taken to the Boston City Hospital.

The Board of Merit hereby announces that the name of Fire Fighter John T. Brignoli, Ladder Company 7 be placed on the Roll of Merit.

JACK BRIGNOLI'S CITATION FROM THE FIREMAN'S BALL PROGRAM. THE WORDS "EXTREME PERSONAL RISK" ARE MISSING!

And Then There's This Medal

For all the medals awarded between 1963 and 1983 - 20 John E. Fitzgerald medals, 20 Walter Scott medals, and 16 Patrick J. Kennedy medals - and while all richly deserved, one stands head and shoulders above the rest.

And lest there be any questions about my opinion versus another's, I canvassed dozens of firemen who worked during this time period and they all agree. To a man, they said the same thing: The feat of stark courage performed by Fire Fighter Bill Shea of the Rescue on January 28, 1966, was unparalleled in their memories.

Now I didn't know Bill Shea in 1966. I didn't meet him until 1971 or so when he made Lieutenant and transferred to Engine 24.

I was fortunate to have worked with him for some time in the early 1970s. He was an exemplary fire officer; a man who knew no fear and never, ever hesitated. Following him was not easy. He made decisions on the spot and they were always correct. He went places that not everyone wanted to go - or could go. Yet, he never put us in a position where we'd get hurt - beyond the regular hazards of the profession, that is. There was an incident shortly after he arrived; before we knew him very well and, so, knew what to expect at a fire. Two firemen were climbing a back stairway in a three decker heading for the fire on the top floor. The hallway was pretty smoky, the plaster ceilings were falling down on top of them (as they always did) and the closer they got to the fire floor, naturally, the hotter it got. They reached the rear doorway that lead into the kitchen. The fire was roaring out and into the hallway.

Then, just before they crawled toward the door, nozzle aimed and ready to do battle, one asked the other, "Where's the Lieutenant?" You see, we were accustomed to having the boss right there with us, telling us what to do.

"I don't know," came the casual reply.

So, on they went, crawling and moving forward. They entered the room, turned the 1½-inch line loose and it darkened down pretty quickly. There was still more fire ahead of them, so they started to crawl through the kitchen and head for the other rooms.

All of a sudden, one yelled, "Hey, Loo! What the hell are you doing here?"

They both shook their heads in disbelief. There sat Lieutenant Bill Shea, back against the wall, knees up, arms leaning on his knees, waiting for them.

"Oh, I knew you'd get here eventually," he replied with a grin.

After having talked to many former firemen about what he did these many years ago at the Paramount Hotel in downtown Boston, I decided I wanted to get the story right from the horse's mouth. When Bill Noonan and I arrived at Bill Shea's home in suburban Boston, he greeted me with his patented, vise-like hand shake. (Some things never change.)

Frankly, I expected him to downplay his contribution. I wasn't disappointed.

Author: Tell me about the Paramount hotel fire. January 1966.

Bill Shea: Didn't know what we were going to when we responded. We were sent to a regular alarm for a pulled box. When we pulled down Washington Street, we saw this great big expanse. No sidewalks or anything. Blown right out through there. I can remember seeing a sailor draped over a balcony in the front of the building. He was gonzo. And there was a guy standing in the front door. But he couldn't get ... he had thirty feet of open space blown out of the sidewalk and the street. We pulled in and we grabbed a ground ladder and threw it across the sidewalk to span what was open. And then we got, I think, a Coca-Cola sign. It was a long one; it was twenty feet long and laid that on the rungs so that you could more or less, if you were careful, you could walk across.

So we went across and got the guy out the entrance way to the Paramount Hotel. And when we got to him, he told us, "They're dying in there!" There was really nothing showing. And there weren't even huge amounts of fire. It was an explosion. Everything had blown itself out. I remember that Frank took the guy that we picked from the doorway to bring him out, and I went in. It was all marble and everything, a beautiful entryway. Pretty fancy looking. And there's a big hole. I looked down and there's this great big woman down in the pit. And she's looking at me and .... and I was mad at her. I said what the hell, what have you done to me? (laughter) I'm in a spot where I either have to walk away from her or do something. And ... so I ... she was standing on a pile of debris and I jumped down there. And I don't know how I lifted her up.

Author: How far down was it?

Bill Shea: Oh it was about twelve feet, like the space between a first floor and a basement. But it wasn't that far. In fact, actually, when you consider that I jumped on to a pile of rubble, it was probably eight or ten feet. Just beyond what you could reach way out and use your hands to pull yourself out. So I jumped down and got her and I'm crying out like a baby (laughter) c'mon! I'm yelling. But I got her up and . . .

Author: There was no one down there to help

JOHN E. FITZGERALD MEDAL

FOR MOST MERITORIOUS ACT — 1966

is hereby awarded to

FIREFIGHTER WILLIAM D. SHEA

A Member of the Rescue Co.

In recognition of a most extraordinary act of courage displayed during a five alarm fire and explosion in a hotel on Boylston St., Boston, on the evening of January 28, 1966, at which time, Firefighter Shea jumped through a large hole at the first floor level into the basement.

While smoke, fire, gas and explosions surrounded him, he located a trapped woman, raised her up over his head and passed her to other members of the Rescue Co. on the first floor level, thereby saving this woman from certain death in this flaming basement.

In performing this act, Firefighter Shea sustained burns to his face, neck and hands and suffered severely from physical exhaustion.

Bill Shea's citation from the Fireman's Ball program

you pull her out?

Bill Shea: No. But I got her up far enough so she could reach up there and the rest of the company, they…but it's funny how pissed off at her I was for putting me in a spot like this.

Author: And there was fire down there, too, right?

Bill Shea: Oh yeah, yeah. The fire was kind of…the pile of debris was almost like a volcano in the middle and the fire was all around…but it wasn't enough to put you out of commission or anything. The heat was bad. In fact I ended up getting my face burnt a little bit. But mostly it was just outrage that…(voice trails off).

Author: How did you get out?

Bill Shea: Well, I was able to grab the little lip…I assume that one of the guys on the company gave me a hand or something like that. I just, got out of it that way. But I can remember that when they took me out…they sent me to the Massachusetts General Hospital for a check over, and I came right back. Then the Lieutenant from Engine 22 and I were working underground, down in that cellar, and we got several bodies out of that pile of crap that was down there. We never realized exactly how bad a fire it was. I mean I didn't. What we saw…the Chief in command was surely aware about the fire going up the stairs. Some civilian guy got killed in the top floor in his room. And that sailor I saw at the beginning, he was long gone. He was killed right away. I don't know whether he was out on the sidewalk and got blown up there because it was like a bomb had gone off. But we never knew what we were heading for. First hint we got was when we pulled up in front of the building and there's no sidewalk, there's no nothing. But no huge amount of fire, either. Just explosion damage.

Author: How big around was the hole you jumped through?

Bill Shea: Oh, about as big as this room, about what, say, twelve by twelve? That was another night that we had a detailed Lieutenant on the Rescue. He's the one. He wrote it up. And I don't know if he lost his head but he made it sound like it was super colossal, but I was more mad than anything else.

Author: Well, I'll tell you a little story. I've been doing a lot of research for this. I've talked to a lot of people. And I'm going to write something on the subject of medals. How some of them are . . . they're all deserved.

Bill Shea: Yeah.

Author: But there are different versions about what happened at different fires.

Bill Shea: Absolutely.

Author: Your's has been deemed as the most

deserving Fitzgerald Medal of all.

Bill Shea: Well, now, I don't think it was. In fact, I think the best job I ever did on the fire department was never mentioned.

Well, isn't that interesting? The fireman, the almost unanimous choice as the one man who performed the most meritorious act during the 21 years covered by this book, believes the Lieutenant who wrote him up had "lost his head," and that he had actually done his "best job" at another fire but was never recognized. He also down played his contribution. He said "I got my face burnt a little bit."

Right, Bill. But how about your ears? Your hands? How about the years of having trouble with these hands after the fire? How about being off on injured leave - after you went back to the fire and helped - for several weeks while your burns healed?

Sorry, Bill, you're not getting away with this one. You can pooh-pooh your efforts that night and make believe anyone would have done it. But that just isn't true. They'll be talking about you in fire houses a hundred years from now. As well they should.

That was an 8, right?

The fireman on house watch is responsible for several things, not the least of which is making sure the company responds where and when it's supposed to respond. It's not a difficult job as long as you can (1) understand what the fire alarm guys tell you to do; where they're telling you to go and (2) count to ten so that when you listen to the bells you can act accordingly.

Well, most of the time, anyway.

The man on watch heard the warning tone indicating that an alarm of fire was about to be transmitted. He reached for a piece of chalk and prepared to write the numbers on the chalk board secured to the desk in front of him.

●●●●●●●● ●● ● ●●●●●●

That's an easy one....8216.

The fireman knows that the 82 prefix is what they call a mutual aid box; there's a fire in a neighboring city or town. So he pulls the running card from the 8200 file and checks - 8216 is Everett. He finds his company's assignment. On the second alarm, they will respond directly to the fire in Everett. So for now, all is well.

Then, a few minutes later:

·· ········ ·· · ······

Second alarm! That's what the two at the beginning means.

The fireman turns on the house lights and bangs down on the button for the house gong. The fire house springs to life. "Mutual aid to Everett!" he yells.

The driver consults his mental map and decides which route to take. When everyone is aboard, the red lights go on, the boss steps on the siren button and presses down as out the door they go.

Destination: Everett.

Generally, because Boston companies don't respond to nearby locations all that often, they will receive instructions over the radio. This is on their mind as they race toward Everett, half expecting to see the fire from afar.

But this fire must be different.

First of all, they can't see anything and second, they've received no specific orders over the radio. Racing up Broadway, they decide to stop at the Everett fire house at the corner of Broadway and Corey Street to see if they can communicate with the Everett dispatchers and get their orders.

Then it happened. Just before they reach the Everett fire house, the radio comes alive; the bells are ringing again and everyone tilts their head toward the radio to listen.

••• ••••••• •• • ••••••

Wonder what the lieutenant is thinking about now?

Huh? What was that?

A third alarm for sure.

But what's the first number after that three?

A seven, right?

Boy, that sure sounded like 3-7216.

7216 is located at the corner of D and Baxter Streets . . . in South Boston.

We go to that, right?

Maybe.

Maybe, my ass.

I'm positive we go.

But we can't go because we're in Everett, seven miles and twenty minutes away.

We're still looking for the fire in Everett.

But you know what . . . 7216 sure sounds an awful lot like 8216, right?

Hey, wait a cotton pickin' minute!

Is it possible?

Oh, no, I hope not.

But we have to find out.

Busy as Hell

Shut off the lights and siren and drive slowly past the Everett fire house.

Damn, it's dark.

The companies are inside.

It sure doesn't look like there's a big fire in Everett.

Oh, no, here comes the radio again!

••••   •••••••   ••   •   ••••••

A fourth alarm! Do we go?

Of course we do!

Let's sneak back into Boston. Let's check and find out. But where?

We can't go to Ladder 9's house; they'll be home.

Okay, let's do this. Let's go by Engine 50's house.

They head in town on most fires so their fire house will be empty. Let's check their running cards.

Find out what our assignment is.

God, I hope we don't go to the fire.

But I know we do. We're screwed.

Stop. Run inside. Check.

Damn!

We're late!

Step on it!

New Lieutenant - Old Driver

The Lieutenant wasn't new in the way you're thinking. In fact, he'd been on the job a tiny bit longer than the "old driver" and had been a Lieutenant for a number of years. Why, they even knew each other pretty well, having been to many of the same fires over the years since the late 60's. But, the new Lieutenant was new to Ladder 29 and, so, had enough sense to understand that treading carefully was the best way to measure his new crew.

The first test came during the first day tour. Fire Alarm sent Ladder 29 to a non-fire incident in the housing project across the street from their fire house at 975 Blue Hill Avenue. As they rolled out the door and crossed the street, the driver said, "Hey, Loo, I know who this woman is. Can we try something different when we get there?"

"Yeah, sure. How do you know her?"

"Well, she's big. I mean she's humongous! She must weigh 500 pounds if she weighs an ounce."

"Why are we going over there," the Loo asked.

"She pulls this shit every week or two. She gets out of her bed and sits on the floor. Then she calls us and says she fell down. She wants to go to the hospital. Her son told me that she does it on purpose when she gets pissed at him."

"She looking for attention, you mean?"

"That's exactly it. She keeps us there for an hour, making believe she can't get up. Then after she's had enough attention, and after a lot of pushing and pulling on our part, she gets back on the bed and we go home."

The Lieutenant laughed. "What do you have in mind?"

"I'll tell you when we get there, okay? You'll see why."

"Okay."

They arrived in a minute or two and immediately went into the large woman's apartment through the dining room and into the bedroom. She was, as the driver predicted, sitting on the bedroom floor with a huge scowl on her face. She was not a happy camper.

The driver caught the Lieutenant's eye and winked. "Loo, can I talk to you out in the hallway?" he asked, loudly.

The Lieutenant, playing along, said, "Sure."

Both men walked out into the hallway and stood next to the door.

Then, in a very loud voice so he'd surely be heard, the driver said: "Loo, I know you're new here so maybe we can suggest another method to get her some help."

"Okay, I'm all ears," the Loo said equally as loud.

"What we should do is go down to the truck, get the long refrigerator straps, they're eight feet long, bring them up here and wrap them around her ass. Then we should drag her across the floor and into the hallway."

By now the Lieutenant is laughing like hell.

The driver continued, "Then, when we get her all the way down the hallway and reach the stairs, we should drag her all the way down to the ambulance one step at a time, and there's twenty-seven steps, I counted, and when we get her to the bottom, put all of our feet on her ass, there's five of us with steel-toed shoes, and then push her up so she can get into the ambulance."

"Sounds good," the lieutenant offered. "What's next?"

"Okay, before we get the refrigerator straps, we should go back in and tell her what we're planning."

"Good. Let's do it."

The two old friends went back into the apartment and guess what?

Yup, she was sitting on her bed, happy as a clam. She told them she was fine. They never heard from her again.

There Were Deputies ....
And Then There Was George

Deputy Fire Chiefs are a singular breed. As the highest non-political rank obtainable through the civil service system, there are fewer deputies than any other rank. They're rather like three-star admirals in the Navy.

Traditionally, there are thirteen Deputy Chiefs in the table of organization; eight are assigned to fire suppression forces duty in either Division 1 or Division 2 while the remaining five work in the various divisions at headquarters; personnel, planning and logistics, training, etc. Those who work in the field are in command of roughly one-half of the city of Boston during their tour of duty.

As one would expect, like all walks of life, each deputy has his own penchants and (let's call them) quirks. Their personalities required that business be conducted a certain way, which meant that we were always aware of the requirements of working with Deputy Chief A as opposed to Deputy Chief B.

Some were what we called Screamers, as in, never be calm, cool, and collected when it's possible to yell, holler, stammer and generally act like a oversexed bantam rooster on steroids.

We had the strong silent types, gentlemen firemen who said enough to get the messages across but did so with an outward sense of calm. They were the best kind of deputy chiefs to work for. The aforementioned Leo Stapleton of Division 1 was one of these.

Some didn't like certain fire companies and their firemen, especially when they came from the other division, while some chiefs loved whoever the hell showed up to help put out their fire.

Some thought they were the cat's ass - others suffered no such pretense.

Taken as a group, they were all good, every one of them. Some were better than others, yes, but as a group, they were good and we were lucky to have them. However, thinking back on it, it isn't difficult to single out one or two deputy chiefs as being just a bit out of the mainstream.

For instance, I once went to the Deputy's office in Division 2 with a request for a special vacation from one of the firefighters on my group.

The chief asked why he wanted the special vacation.

I told him the firefighter's wife was expecting their first child on a certain date and he wanted to be there for the birth and to help his wife when she came home with the baby.

The chief disapproved the request.

Just like that: "No."

I knew enough not to ask why and walked out of his office trying to figure out what the chief's problem was and, then, even worse, how to break the bad news to the expectant father. It wasn't easy, but there was really only one way to do it - I just said "He disapproved it."

Well, for the next half hour or so the guys were beside themselves. They called that chief everything under the sun, and, frankly, I probably called him a few choice names myself.

A while later, as I was walking past the chief's door, he stopped me. "Do you want to know why I said no?" he asked.

"I'd love to know why," I replied, as stoically as I could.

"My experience has been that a woman, especially with the first pregnancy, will very often deliver later than her due date. So tell him this, tell him I disapproved the request for a certain set of dates right now because his wife could be late giving birth. But, as soon as she has the baby, I will put him on vacation right then and there. That way he won't give away valuable vacation time. He can get the time, the full two weeks, when he actually needs it, not when he thinks he might need it."

So there it was - I wasted no time bringing the information back to the fledgling father and the rest of the group, all of whom were still steaming. When I explained the deputy chief's reasoning, they all saw the difference. They forgave him in their minds and went about their business. But one of them said something I had been thinking.

Why the hell would he do that? Why wouldn't he explain his reasoning right up front? Of course, I didn't know the answer. The chief certainly knew he could have explained himself right up front but, in the final analysis, I suspected that he just didn't care what anyone thought of him. By contrast, there was another chief in the same division - Deputy Fire Chief John "Red" Harrison - who, and I'm sure of this, would have seen the request when I gave it to him, told me to go get the fireman and bring him in the office, where he would have told him to take a seat and listen while the chief explained why it was best to wait to submit a special request. I had the good fortune to work on Red's group for several years, four of which were spent on Engine 42, right there in his division headquarters in Egleston Square.

One story comes to mind, the telling of which will prove that the Ol' Redhead didn't worry about a hell of a lot. See, he'd spent his entire career on the city's busiest engine and ladder companies and, so, developed a somewhat stoic command presence. On the night in question, Engine 42 was first due to what turned out to be a working fire in an old abandoned factory on Terrace Street. When we arrived, fire was showing in several windows on the top floor. We humped a big line up the stairs - it took a few minutes - and started putting water on the fire. We were soon joined by members of Ladder 30 (RIP) and District Chief Frank Linso. Frank was a hell of a guy, a real gentleman. He found us fifty or so feet inside the door and moving forward; there was fire everywhere. Chief Linso tapped me on the shoulder and said, "Mike, I'll stay with your men, go down and tell the boss we need another big line up here. Maybe two." (This was before we had portable radios.) There's no arguing with a chief and you just go and do what he tells you. I made it down to the street and found the Deputy.

"Chief, Chief Linso said we need another big line up there. Maybe two."

Chief Harrison nodded and turned to the officer of the engine company standing ready for orders. "Cap, take your big line and follow Lieutenant Foley upstairs. He'll hand you off to Chief Linso."

"Okay, Chief," the Captain answered.

The Captain and I nodded to one another and I turned to leave.

"Mike!" the Redhead yelled.

"Chief," I replied, turning back.

Now you have to picture the scene - here's the backdrop: there's a five-story building with fire roaring out ten windows and coming through the roof. Ladders are going up, lines are being run, pumps roar, and the Division Commander, who is standing in the middle of the street suddenly takes up his golf stance!

"Today, I wasn't hitting the ball square."

Red goes into his backswing.

"Goddamned thing was all over the place."

Red starts his downswing.

"Too many slices. Any ideas?"

Now what the hell am I supposed to say? Not much. All I could do was blurt out, "You're shitting me, right Chief?"

Red roared with laughter and with the big smile of his said, "Okay, go. We'll talk back in the fire house."

Also for consideration is the deputy chief who seemed friendly and personable enough but who could be an acerbic, arrogant bastard.

His public smack down moment - and to make it, oh, so delicious, it was self inflicted - came when he exercised a non-existent discretion of his exalted deputyship over the fire radio and countermanded an order given by a fire fighter senior man who asked for more help when he arrived at a fire.

The senior man of a ladder company arrived at a fire ahead of everyone else and sizing up the situation, told Fire Alarm, "This is a working fire."

His Royal Deputyship, who wasn't even near the fire yet, screamed into the radio, "Cancel that working fire!"

Fire Alarm did as the deputy said and for reasons known only to themselves; the SOP is very clear on who is in command at a fire, and in this instance, being first on the scene, it was the senior firefighter.

Then in what would become page #1 material in the Eat Your Own Words Manual of Operations, when His Royal Deputyship finally arrived at the fire, he had to lower his voice and order not just the second alarm but the third and fourth and fifth alarms, too.

In other words, the fire fighter senior man had asked for one additional engine company while the deputy, after a veritable feast of his own words were unceremoniously shoved down his throat, called for 16 additional engine companies to put the fire out. There wasn't a fireman in the city who didn't revel in His Royal Deputyship's very public and wholly self-imposed comeuppance. He put himself in his own place. Ha!

By contrast, there was a similar incident at a different time in District 7 where a fire fighter senior man did the same thing, reported a working fire. For some reason - no one had ever heard this before - Fire Alarm called the responding commander, District Chief Vin Bolger, and asked him if it was okay. Bolger replied, "I'm not there. He is. Better do what he says."

While there were variables to their personalities and methods, there is one deputy chief who stands head and shoulders above them all, and for many various reasons: George Thompson.

He is the only deputy who struck fear into the hearts and minds of some of his subordinates, and I'm talking about shake-in-your-boots fear.

He is the only deputy chief who had what can only be described as a nickname that crossed between intentionally disparaging and one of high honor hung around his neck, one that stuck like glue.

George Thompson was known as King George, though to my knowledge, never to his face and never to be confused with George III of England, the monarch who lost a Revolutionary War to the colonists. In fact, Great Britain's King George was a silk pants wearing, candy-ass mama's boy compared to the BFD's King George.

He was a mainstay presence in Division 1 for fourteen years from 1965 through 1979 and he stands out from the rest; if for no other reason than he was aloof, unapproachable, and the owner of a commanding presence who didn't suffer fools. Of course, we had no idea how he interacted with the other deputy chiefs. For all we knew, he was an amiable guy who loved to drink Chivas Regal and tell dirty jokes. Frankly, I'd always hoped he was a different kind of guy in his regular life, different from he was in the persona he presented to most of us: distant, antisocial, and downright unfriendly.

King George believed in (and used) a strong chain of command with unalterable firmness and passion. At fires, he rarely, if ever, spoke to anyone but a subordinate district chief or a company officer who reported to him at the front of a building on fire. There is also ample evidence to support the notion that he didn't talk to subordinates very much at all, even in the fire house. He lacked the common touch, the kind of superior-to-minion interaction you've seen portrayed in movies and, if you're lucky, in real life when the military generals or admirals stop along their busy routes and talk with the privates and corporals. Personally, I only had a few direct dealings with George and never ran afoul of his orders. As a result, I never felt his wrath. So, maybe I'm not the perfect analyst to offer a conclusion about why he was the way he was.

Deputy Fire Chief George F. Thompson - "King George." He's laughing because Bill Noonan just told him that by wearing his dress uniform to a fire, he looked like General Patton.

DEPUTY FIRE CHIEF JOHN R. HARRISON "THE REDHEAD"

MIKE FOLEY

DEPUTY FIRE CHIEF
GEORGE F. THOMPSON -
ALWAYS IN COMMAND

But I do know it was revealed after he died that he had told his family that he did not want the fire department notified of his death until some two weeks had passed. Had the department been notified as per usual, they would have announced his death over the radio, and I am convinced that George didn't want that to happen because he knew he wasn't well thought of and feared that people would show up at his wake just to make sure he was dead and then, later, to visit his grave and provide a human element to the task of keeping the grass green? There isn't any way to verify this notion - and I will happily be corrected if someone can do so - but it seems to square with what little I knew of him and what became the legend that surrounded him.

King George was a hard, tough task master but a highly efficient and extremely capable fire officer. You always knew where you stood with him. He ran fires as though he was conducting an orchestra. There wasn't any fanfare or razzle-dazzle; he just knew every musician in his band and how, when, and where to use the instruments they brought along with them. He had a picture in his mind of what the building looked like and where everyone was. If he sent a company to the third floor rear, well, by God that's where they better go - and remain. He didn't tolerate any free lancing or interpretation of his orders. He told you what to do and expected you to do it, nothing more, nothing less. This sounds pretty simple, especially if you've ever been in the military, right? I mean, who didn't follow his orders? Well, the answer is, "some people." But believe me, they only did it once.

There were some who believed that the deputy was too rigid in his demands - that he discouraged aggressive fire fighting in favor of having to know where everyone was - and on at least one occasion they tested his willingness to re-think his orders. (Just thinking about it makes me laugh.)

Anyway, there's a story about a certain engine company that was ordered to take their line into the second floor of a certain section of the fire building. They did so but, alas, didn't find any fire. In short order though, they saw an adjacent section of the building burning freely. This was the perfect opportunity. Would King George want them to stay put or would he appreciate their enthusiasm and thank them for putting the fire out in the area they had seen? The Lieutenant, egged on by his young crew, decided to take the chance. At first blush, it seemed like a good idea. They crawled through a window and entered the adjacent area of the building. Then they had a field day with their big line, pouring water onto a large area of fire. Naturally, the fire darkened down to the point where the absence of fire was noticeable from the outside.

Yes, outside.

Where King George was standing tall, in complete command.

He immediately summoned his aide and told him to find out why the fire had darkened down so quickly and, if someone was there against his orders, to have the officer report to him immediately. You see, what the enthusiastic engine crew didn't know was that King George had sent an engine company into that area not two minutes before.

In other words, King George knew there was no way they were already inside and operating. It was impossible.

The only answer then, was the correct one. Another company had gone there without being told to do so.

There'd be hell to pay.

The aide entered the room where the engine company was having so much fun and found the Lieutenant. "My God, Loo, what the hell are you doing?" he asked. "The boss is pissed. He wants to see you outside, right now."

There is no record of the conversation. But there was a result; one we felt the next time we went to a fire in Division 1.

Upon arrival at a three alarm fire in South Boston,

the Lieutenant reported to King George and was ordered to hook up to a hydrant with our front suction, run two lines, each over 300-feet in length, to put them into Engine 26's pump, and fill both lines, ostensibly to supply them with needed water.

We got the job done in good time and prepared ourselves for action.

Then, while we stood a safe distance away, the Lieutenant reported to King George that the task had been completed.

"Stand by right there," King George ordered, turning around and pointing to a piece of the street twenty some feet away.

The Lieutenant moved to the spot and stood there.

By himself.

For an hour.

Finally, after King George decided the Lieutenant had been there long enough - there was still 600-feet feet of hose filled with water, connected and never used - he ordered him to shut down the pump, disconnect the hose, drain the water, roll up the hose, and go home.

So there it was: King George's Revenge.

Yet, despite the reputation as the quintessential hard ass, there seems to be at least one instance when he made a complete and utter ass of himself in the fire house and responded with a loud belly laugh and shockingly so, right in front of everyone, privates included.

Legend has it that George, while still a District Chief in District 7, for some odd reason, was looking over Engine 17's pump. Now, at the time, about 1965, every engine company fireman in America knew that the suction connection has two gates and that both accepted supply lines - feeder lines - from a hydrant. They also knew that unless you wanted to get drenched, the gates should only be opened when the supply hose is connected.

So you can imagine when King George, a former Captain of the very busy Engine 23, who absolutely should have known better, and who was in his full dress uniform, walked over the suction connection on Engine 17's pump and opened the gate. He was instantly soaked! As luck (good luck or bad luck, depending on who you were) would have it, there were several people standing around, mostly just rank and file firefighters. As soon as he opened the gate and the water came out, he reacted by jumping back and trying to close the gate. They say that everyone was shocked at the enormity of his mistake and did their level best not to laugh out loud.

He quickly pushed the gate closed and stopped the water. Then, realizing what he had done and what form of audience he had, he turned around and said, "Well that was a pretty stupid thing to do."

Then he laughed! A genuine belly laugh.

Shaking his head in disbelief and probably realizing that he had just let his guard down and displayed a little self depreciation, he readjusted his outward persona, walked away, and went upstairs to change his clothes.

Welcome to where the rest of us live, King!

But overall, it really didn't matter a whole lot to us whether the deputy was friendly or approachable or a back-slapping nice guy. We wanted a guy who knew what he was doing and who would look out for us, take care of us. And for every fireman who thought King George was a pompous-ass, no personality idiot, there are hundreds and hundreds who believed - who knew - he was a damn fine boss.

You may count me among the latter.

Swapping Tours

"Can you work for me next Wednesday night?"

"Sure."

"Great. Thanks. I owe you a tour. Anytime you want me to repay it, I'm there."

"Sounds good."

In general terms, that kind of firehouse conversation took place thousands of times during the war years. While the words may have been different, the substance of the agreement was always the same: if you get someone to work for you, you pay them back when they ask you to; if you owed someone a tour and they asked you to work for them, you always said yes - even if you already had something planned. And, if that was the case, then it was your job to then find someone else to work the tour in question. The only consideration for the parties involved was that the fireman who was owed the tour was off duty. Period.

Of course there was always room for creativity.

One evening, in a fairly busy firehouse, the oncoming night tour firemen were gathered in the kitchen. They exchanged the usual pleasantries and lamented the latest Red Sox loss. But, on this particular night there was an additional man seated at the table. No one knew who he was. He sat alone, didn't speak, and slowly sipped his coffee. Finally, one of the bosses came into the kitchen and asked whether anyone had seen a certain fire fighter.

"Haven't seen him, Loo."

"Nope. Is he in the locker room?"

"I've looked everywhere. He's not here," the Loo replied.

The unidentified man looked up and answered, "I'm working for him."

"Huh? What?" the Loo asked. "Who the hell are you?"

"Uh, my name is Walter."

"Walter? Walter who? What company are you from? How come I don't know anything about this? You're not on my company. Again, what company are you from?"

"I work at the post office."

By now, everyone is interested in the conversation. The firemen start to laugh. The Loo is incredulous.

"The post office?! What the hell is going on here? Are you even a fireman?

"No, I'm a mailman."

The room erupts in laughter. The Loo cannot help himself; he laughs, too.

"A mailman? You're a mailman?"

"Yup. My friend works here. He's a fireman. He asked me if I could work for him tonight. He's goin' somewhere with his girl. He told me that he'd work for me at the post office next Saturday."

"Go home."

"I don't have to work?"

"No, you don't. Go home."

"Aw, shit. I was lookin' forward to riding on a fire engine with all the sirens and shit."

"Take the night off and don't breathe a word of this to your friend."

"Ah, okay."

Then the Loo took care of the situation. He found a day tour fireman who hadn't left yet and asked if he could help out by working for the certain fireman. "I owe you one," the Loo told the day tour fireman.

But the Loo never told the certain fireman that he didn't have to work at the post office on Saturday.

The Not-So-Good Humor Man

One fine summer day, we were sitting on the bench in front of the fire house in Grove Hall. It was early evening, about 6:30 or so. We'd already been out a few times, chasing false alarms.

Then we saw an ice cream truck weaving down Washington Street. Surely, the driver was drunk on his ass, so we kind of laughed and made a few comments. "Hey, check this out. Guy's drunk," someone said.

Well, we're not cops so we didn't plan to do anything about trying to stop this moving hazard looking for a place to crash. It had nothing to do with us. Well, until the driver suddenly turned the wheel hard to the left, aimed for Ladder 23's door and then stopped just short of crashing.

One of the guys yelled, "Hey! Get that goddamned thing out of here! This is a firehouse you idiot!"

The driver started to get out and, yeah, he looked like he was well oiled. Someone yelled again, "Hey, asshole! Move!"

The driver didn't make a motion to move his truck. Instead, he fell out of his seat and landed right there on the apron in front of the overhead door. We got up and walked over still figuring the guy was hammered.

We leaned over.

"Hey! Get up!"

"Someone shot me," he said.

"What?! Shot you?"

"Yes, they shot me twice and robbed me."

What can you say, besides "Ooooops."

Paperwork

It's been said that paperwork will slow an attacking army to a crawl. The incomparable Lewis B. Puller, Lieutenant General, USMC, was known to have hated paperwork so much that when he was asked by a new XO about the status of the communiques he'd received from division headquarters he patted his right hip pocket and said, "This is the out box," and then, patting his left hip pocket added, "this is the in box." When asked why his "in box" was empty, he replied, "Never kept any of 'em, never missed any." He believed that the people writing those messages - rear-echelon planners who commanded only their desks - had precious little understanding of what was going on at the front lines, and, so, deserved to be ignored. He was right of course, and by discarding all that paper and the messages contained thereon, General Puller invented the most efficient filing system ever devised; he read precious few and kept none.

But paperwork can be fun. No, really.

Consider these examples.

A young fireman entered the company office and asked the Lieutenant if he could put a paper in and get transferred to another company. The officer said, yes, he could do that. The conversation went something like this:

"How do I do it, Loo?"

"I'll type it for you. But why do you want to leave?"

"I want to be closer to my family."

"Oh, okay. I get it. Where do you want to go?"

"Birmingham."

"Birming-what? Did you say Birmingham?"

"Yeah, Birmingham."

"Ah, most people request a certain company. Most people specify a certain engine company, or maybe a ladder company. I don't understand Birmingham."

"I want to go to Birmingham, Alabama."

The Lieutenant knew he heard correctly and tried to conceal his amusement. "Ah, I can type it and send it in, but I wouldn't hold my breath if I were you. I don't know of any transfers made to other states."

"That's okay. I know it's a long shot but I'm willin' to try."

"Okay then."

The Lieutenant started typing the paper:

I request that I be transferred from my present assignment . . .

"Which engine or ladder in Birmingham?"

"I don't care. I don't know any of them."

"Okay, I'll write 'any available company.'"

In short order the request is typed. The Lieutenant removed the paper from the typewriter and said, "Sign right here."

The fireman signed the paper, thanked the boss, and left.

Pretty funny, huh?

Oh, it gets better.

The Lieutenant flipped the paper over, signed the Captain's name - therefore approving the request - and put it in the out box. He knew that the District Chief would pick it up the next morning.

Pretty funny, huh?

Oh, it gets better.

The District Chief signed the paper and therefore approved the request. He then gave the paper to the Deputy Chief who also signed it and, therefore, approved the request. Obviously, neither of them read it. Result? It went all the way to headquarters.

About two weeks later, the Lieutenant arrived at work to relieve the Captain.

"Got a call from Personnel this morning," the Captain said with a grin, "Seems I approved a transfer request. One of your guys wants to go to any company in Birmingham, Alabama. I don't remember signing anything like that."

The Lieutenant couldn't fake it. "You didn't sign

it. I did. I didn't want to bother you with it. I'm just amazed that it was signed and approved all the way along the line and wound up in Personnel."

"If it's any consolation, the chief in Personnel was laughing his ass off. He said it was the funniest thing he'd seen in a long time."

But this Lieutenant wasn't finished. Nope.

A while later he decided to once again test the system to see just how much attention anyone paid to the papers that flowed back and forth from headquarters or, as we often called it, Disneyland.

This time the target was a form 5D, the standard form used to report an injury.

In filling out the form, it was necessary to include the usual, basic information: name, rank, company, etc. But, there was also a place for a narrative, and to satisfy the requirement the officer has two choices: I observed/it was reported to me

He can either say he actually saw what happened or XX that out and leave the "it was reported to me" part.

Here, in part, is what the Lieutenant wrote:

Name: Blackie T. Cat

Rank: Feline

Narrative: It was reported to me that while rounding a corner and starting to walk down the hallway, Feline Cat saw a little mouse scurrying across the floor headed for the boiler room. Feline Cat immediately gave chase. However, while in pursuit and while traveling at top speed, Feline Cat turned sharp left and ran into the boiler room where he tripped over a discarded and empty Marlboro crush proof box and then fell heavily to the floor, injuring his shoulder. Feline Cat remained on duty and will seek medical attention at Dr. Wolf's Animal Hospital on River Street at the completion of his tour of duty.

Witnesses: Rin Tin Tin; Lassie

Well, guess what?

Yup.

The injury paper on a fictitious cat named Blackie, complete with its silly narrative describing an imaginary injury, was signed and approved by at least two chiefs and - unless it's been purged - I'm guessing it has been - still sits in the department's archives.

In conclusion, there are (or were) at least a dozen other papers of similar variety, not the least of which was a report signed, approved, and forwarded by, and I quote:

Quido Sarducci, Fire Lieutenant, SNL

The Parting Of The Seas

When someone pulls a fire box that is located on the sidewalk, usually at an intersection, the nearest engine and ladder are sent to investigate. In residential areas, the fire engines arrive at the location of the alarm box, look around the immediate neighborhood and decide whether there's a reason for the alarm. If there's a fire, naturally, the companies will call for more help. But, if there's isn't anything showing, they report a false alarm and return to quarters. Generally, the entire false alarm process, from time of arrival at a location until the companies leave is a minute or two, or less.

However, when a fire box is pulled inside a larger building - like, for instance, a Boston University dormitory on Commonwealth Avenue - the firemen have to enter the building and check every floor. It's a royal pain in the butt because everyone knows it's a false alarm - even the students. But in their all-to familiar ritual, the eight or ten firemen divide into teams of two and do their job, floor by floor, room by room.

On a cold winter night, made even more delicious by something the weather people call a wintery mix of rain and sleet, some knucklehead decided to disturb the entire student population - some 600 strong - located inside an 18 story dormitory. He or, yes, she, pulled the alarm box and set into motion what was soon to become an unfortunate series of events for one particular wise-ass student, a mental midget who didn't have the brains to keep his big mouth shut.

The clacker box alarm resonated through the fire house - it sounded like a chicken being run over by an Abrams tank - the gang at Engine 33 and Ladder 15 jogged for the apparatus, climbed aboard, started putting their gear on, and after learning their destination, headed out the door into miserable weather, turned right and drove off into the night, red lights flashing, sirens wailing, air horns blasting.

Destination - 700 Commonwealth Avenue.

The BU dorm.

Again.

Third time tonight.

Grrrrrr!

As the companies approached, the scene that lay before them was very different from the two previous times. Usually, the building empties out and the students, all 600 of them, linger in front of the building waiting for the firemen to let them go back inside.

Not this time, though. Nope.

Instead, the students, those who even bothered to leave their rooms, were jammed into the lobby. It was pretty obvious that at least 400 had refused to evacuate and were still inside.

So the Lieutenant decided to give the students a little taste of their own medicine.

You want inconvenience? You got it. You want pain in the ass? Here you go. He told the firemen to evacuate the building. The whole thing. All 18 floors.

Was the measure punitive? Absolutely. It was also by the book. I'll bet that had this been the first run to the dorm this particular night, the boss may have let the students remain in the lobby. So, for the next forty minutes or so, the firemen checked every room on every floor. They ordered everyone outside suggesting that they bring their coats along. When they were sufficiently convinced that there was no fire and that alarm was false, they started down the stairs to leave. When they reached the lobby, they sort of marched in a group toward the large front door. When the first fireman in line opened the door, the students didn't move. It was an odd moment.

Remember we talked about the mental midget who didn't have the brains to keep his big mouth shut? Well, here comes his cue . . .

One of the firemen said to the group of students immediately blocking the door, which included said big mouth, "Excuse me."

Well, instead of moving; Big Mouth raised his fist and said, "Fuckin' asshole firemen!"

He never saw it coming.

A short left jab delivered Ladder 15 style, by an ex-Golden Gloves pugilist.

Boom! Right on the chin.

Big Mouth went down like a tree struck by lightning.

And then, a miracle! 600 students parted like the Red Sea.

Moses would have been proud.

Death Rides Along

Ours is a somber business. Death rides along with us everywhere we go. And this isn't just a casual adage chroniclers and poets use to describe a dangerous occupation, the message that says, "You never know whether a <fill in the occupation> will come home from work." Of course, yes, it's true, you don't know who will come home safe and sound and who will not. For verification's sake, consider that thirty-eight Boston firemen lost their lives during the years this book covers, i.e., 1963-1983. The same bit of prophetic alert can be offered to anyone, in any line of work. Yes, firemen die; but so do airline pilots, cops, restaurant owners, fishermen, artists, event planners, pizza shop owners, house painters, and shoe shine boys. Eventually, death comes for all of us though, generally, before it does, firemen see more of it than the average person. And more than usually, it's the civilians who do the dying . . .

BRIGHTON

January 1976.

Sunday morning.

First alarm transmitted at 0607 hours.

Then ... the kind of radio traffic that tells the story.

Urgency in the voice of the otherwise placid District Fire Chief.

0609 hours: Working fire.

0610 hours: Second alarm.

That's us.

Our assignment is to cover the first due ladder company. The crew of Ladder 15 is not even out of the fire house yet. But we already know. All the ingredients are there.

Thickly populated area of Brighton.

Time of day.

This isn't good.

People are dying. Or already dead.

At some point - I don't remember when - we were dispatched to the fire as an extra truck. It seemed like a long ride that morning, three point one miles if you believe Google maps, which I do. Each man is alone with his thoughts because, like I said, we already knew what awaited us.

By the time we arrived, the fire was pretty much out. The guys from those Brighton companies did one hell of a job that morning.

They got inside quickly and kicked the fire's ass.

They rescued people over ladders.

But their frantic efforts were mostly for naught, because even arriving as quickly as they did, it was already too late.

Six precious souls from one family would perish that winter morning.

They were 20, 12, 8, 6, 4 and 8 months young.

When we arrived, our Lieutenant reported to the Deputy Chief who ordered our crew into the second floor to help with the overhauling.

"We're looking for bodies," the LT quietly told us.

We went over a ground ladder into the second floor. I went first. Three more firemen followed right behind. We stepped through the window and stood silently in the 4-5 inches of water that had accumulated on the floor. There were several other firemen already in the room and we just sort of surveyed everything for a few seconds, looking for a place where we may be needed. One of our crew started walking toward the other side of the room and while sloshing through the water, almost tripped on something. He bent down and picked it up, looked at it, and in a single motion, half-placed and half-tossed it on the bed saying, "It's a doll."

In that instant, my brain reduced events to super slow motion. It was like being outside your own body, watching yourself do something. I watched as the doll went from the fireman's hand and on to the bed, where he'd laid it on its back. It's little arms were out by its side, in the same position they'd be if someone yelled "Stick 'em up!"

Its doll face looked rubbery.

But, no.

No, this wasn't a doll.

It was the missing 8-month old infant.

The fireman who found "the doll" noticed, too. He slowly sat down on the bed and placed his big hand on the tiny body. The rest of us formed a little circle around him and the infant and then bowed our heads - four experienced, reasonably tough firemen, acted as one as we stood vigil, even if only for a fleeting moment, until the stretcher arrived.

While we waited, I glanced down at the jake sitting on the bed beside the baby. His lips, like my own, were moving.

As alluded to above, generally, firemen see more death than the average person. But I was lucky, very lucky. I didn't see near as much as some firemen. In fact, I'd have to believe that I saw much less than my share, if such an analysis is even possible. I know other firemen have similar memories - worse memories, more graphic and cruel, memories of having to go to the morgue and identify a body crushed by a falling building, a body that a few hours before was a walking, talking friend of forty years. Those memories are more horrific than any I can imagine. Yet, for some reason, if I close my eyes right now - as I have done ten thousand times since that Sunday morning - I can still see that little baby. It's as though I am watching a well-rehearsed movie scene in my mind, over and over and over. Death is the producer and director of what haunts my memory.

But I am not alone.

Every fireman has seen too much death, and every fireman sees the same kinds of movies in their mind, over and over, for again, Death rides along with us everywhere we go.

THE INTERSECTION

Summer time.

Early evening.

They heard the collision from the fire house.

Someone from Engine 24 or Ladder 23 called the Fire Alarm office and told them they were responding up the block a few hundred feet to what was surely an automobile accident at one of the area's busiest intersections.

Arriving on the scene in a minute or less, they surveyed the scene before them. At least two and maybe three cars were involved. It didn't take an accident reconstruction team to conclude that someone ran a red light and was hit broadside. As accidents go, this one didn't appear to be anything out of the ordinary.

There was a woman lying in the street. She had almost assuredly been thrown through the windshield because this was before seat belts were used more than every now and then, to say nothing of being mandatory. Her whole body was bloody and her clothes were shredded. One of the firemen stooped down, put his hands under her arms and started to pull her toward the gutter, out of the way of the traffic.

When he gently pulled, her body came apart at the waist.

She was in two pieces.

The fireman blanched and threw up in his mouth.

Then he carefully put her top half back down on the street.

He stood up, removed his helmet and shook his head.

He was a good jake, a terrific guy, and a caring family man. In his mind's eye, I know he did what we all did - he saw his family in the real-life movie that had just played before his eyes. What if that was my wife? My daughter? he thought. He remembered that life is tentative; there are no guarantees. And I know that if he could stand here in front of you right this minute, he'd scream: "Wear your seat belt!"

Only Two Streets Away

As fires go, it was a typical one-roomer.

The first arriving engine was greeted by a large and loud early evening group of spectators milling around on the street and pointing - all of whom were silhouetted by fire that was blowing out one window on the first floor.

The fire engine rolled to a stop. The crew snapped into action and quickly ran an inch-and-a-half line up the cement walkway toward the building, up a short stairway, through the front door, up a few more stairs into the hot and smoke-filled hallway to the first door on the left. The fire was advancing into the hallway, so as best they could, the engine guys ducked down under the fire and smoke and pushed the line into the apartment. Once inside, they took a quick left into the bedroom. Settled in the doorway, the pipe man pulled back on the handle and swung the nozzle back and forth. The fire was out in less than thirty seconds.

The ladder company guys moved in and began to tear the room apart: walls, ceilings, window frames, everything had to be pulled down or apart so they could look for and find the hot spots.

As the smoke lifted, what was left of daylight shone in the room through the window. The bed looked like it was still made up but it was being covered with pulled-down plaster from the ceiling above. Suddenly, the ladder officer noticed something and told everyone to stop what they were doing.

"Oh, my God," he gasped softly while aiming his wheat light at the head of the bed. Everyone followed the singular beam of light as it fell upon a horrifying sight ... a skull sitting on top of an incinerated pillow.

The firemen fell silent.

All work stopped.

The Lieutenant walked to head of the bed, took the bed spread in his hand and slowly, gently pulled it down. Again, he shone his light at what everyone now knew was a body. In an eerie, bone-chilling sort of way, we were transfixed at the sight laid out before our eyes. It was like something out of a horror movie. The body was that of a teenage girl and except where her head had been, she was intact and wholly unaffected by the fire. Fire investigators later surmised that she had fallen asleep while smoking in bed and that the cigarette had ignited the pillow and burned her face away leaving the blankets to protect the rest of her.

I have thought about that young girl many times over the years. Her's was an unfinished life, one filled with such promise but gone in an instant; a terrible tragedy, such a waste. But her death was worse than it was for parents and siblings who face the heart-wrenching loss of a son or brother who is killed in action in combat - and I know about this - because when young Americans go away to fight, to a place where people are trying to kill them, well, you know in your heart that there's a chance they won't be coming back. But when your teenaged daughter goes to sleep in her bed, you don't expect to her die.

To the family the young girl left behind, there was the sudden and immeasurable pain and sorrow that comes with a wake, a funeral, millions of questions, and a lifetime of asking why. Yet, those of us who were there that day - the firemen who did their job, packed up our hose and tools, climbed back aboard the fire engines and went back to the fire house to await the next summons - never had the chance to tell the family how so very sorry they were for being the ones who found this beautiful young soul. Perhaps they would have taken some comfort in knowing that the ride back to the fire house, and the hours that filled the rest of our day, were survived in utter silence as each of us, alone with our own brand of sadness and grief, tried to cope with same question . . . why?

The Silent Treatment

He arrived as a near brand new Lieutenant early in 1970. Anyone who knows him and worked with him, then reads this book will heartily agree: he was one of the very best fire fighting officers the BFD ever produced. He was polite and unassuming, a soft-spoken man who seldom showed emotion but who attacked fires with a vengeance; he lead by example and always, always! from the front. Despite the outward persona, there wasn't a timid bone in his body and rest assured, he knew his business. With great affection and respect, he was dubbed Clark Kent, you know, "a mild-mannered Fire Lieutenant from a great metropolitan fire department"?

Yet, there were those who believed that he was a pushover because, well, he looked more like a college professor than a fireman. I suppose it was the eye glasses that fooled then because he wore them all the time. But like Clark Kent used to do in the phone booth when he changed into his Superman suit (or is it a costume?), he always removed his glasses at the door, just before he entered any fire building: "None of us can see worth a damn where we're going, anyway," he used to say.

Did I mention that he was soft spoken? Yes, I did, which means that he never raised his voice, not one decibel - not even when all hell was breaking loose at a fire, a time when some officers fall to pieces before your eyes. In fact, he spoke so softly that the Fire Alarm guys used to make him repeat himself, "Say again, Engine 24." Finally, he got ticked off at being asked, so he decided he just wouldn't use the radio anymore: "I'm done talking to those people."

We all laughed like hell because it was so him, so funny. We knew he'd play games with them for a while by letting the drivers talk on the radio, something we almost never did. It was kind of fun for us, too, so we were having a hell of a time. Well, this went on for a tour of duty or two. We'd get a run, arrive at the scene and he would look at us, nod toward the hand set, meaning we should call off.

Then one night it happened. Fire Alarm called us on the inside phone with a message of some urgency and off we went. When we left quarters, we knew we had a fire. You could feel it in your bones. You could smell it in the air. In a minute or two, we arrived.

Fire was roaring out of several windows on two floors. The driver's thoughts are on finding a hydrant and a place to park the fire engine so it won't block the front of the building and, so, screw up ladder company operations. But just as he was ready to jump out of the front seat and get the pump working, the hopelessly laconic Lt. Clark Kent leaned over and, pointing at the transmitter, said, "You gonna tell 'em we're here?"

We liked to say that Lieutenant Clark Kent was so cool that if he went to Key West in July, it would snow.

¿HABLAS ESPAÑOL?

At some point in the early 1970s, the department decided that it would be a good idea for firemen to learn a few important Spanish phrases. The obvious intention was that we should probably be able to communicate with any non-English speaking people (mostly Puerto Rican) we may encounter, especially during emergencies.

They set up informal classes in the firehouses; instructors taught us to say things like No salte! (Don't jump!); ¿Dónde está el fuego? (Where's the fire?);¿Que piso? (What floor?); and Mantenga la calm! (Stay calm.)

Everyone attended and learned as much Spanish as they could. Well sort of.

The first definitive test came a short time later when on a cold December 4, 1971, box 1735 was transmitted at 0237 hours for a fire in a large, five-story brick apartment building situated at the corner of Dudley and Magnolia Streets. The first arriving companies were confronted with a horrifying reality.

There was an awful lot of fire.

There was a whole lot of smoke.

The building, and old hotel, housed some 400 people.

A mass of humanity was streaming down the stairs, into the street.

At least a hundred people were hanging out different windows on all five floors.

Almost none of them spoke English.

At 0239, only two minutes after the first alarm, a second alarm was ordered.

Two additional trucks were also ordered, making a total of six.

That's right, within only 120 seconds, six ladder companies were on the way.

Hundreds of people running around, screaming.

Rapid-fire sounds of excited Spanish phrases filled the air.

It was an absolute mad house.

Ground ladders were flying up all over the place.

As though moving in sync with a symphony orchestra, aerial ladders were plucking people from windows, three or four or five at a time.

However, within sixty minutes, the crisis had passed.

The main body of fire had been knocked down.

Over 125 people were quickly rescued over ladders.

Once again, Boston's ladder company jakes had done the seemingly impossible.

It's no small miracle that only one person perished.

Then, through the chaos and turmoil, the legend and lore of the BFD was confirmed.

It was an event for the ages.

It seems that one of the company officers, fresh from his basic conversation Spanish class, stood in the middle of Dudley Street, and while everything around him was going to hell in a hand basket, confidently hollered to the Spanish people hanging from the windows:

"No jumpo! No jumpo!"

Larry Talbot Lives

Don't know who Larry Talbot is?

Well, you're not alone. There isn't a sliver of one percent of the population who knows who Larry Talbot is - or was.

So, for the record, let me tell you that Lawrence Talbot - I call him Larry - was a character played by Lon Chaney in the 1941 flick, The Wolf Man.

A fictional character.

Or was he?

For years, there were rumors that Larry Talbot lived in the attic of the fire house at 434 Warren Street - Engine 24's old quarters. As the legend claims, he'd been there since just before World War II. He was very quiet, didn't bother anyone, and to our knowledge, never came out of his secret berth in the attic. Of course, we always surmised that he snuck out while we were off fighting fires but if he did, he never left a trace. So far as we were concerned, Larry Talbot lived up there while we lived down here, an unacknowledged though peaceful coexistence.

But then, in the fall of 1972, everything changed.

Apparently, Larry decided that after being cooped up in the attic for thirty plus years, he needed some fresh air - or needed to see live people again. So, one night he quite brazenly abandoned his attic hideaway and started hanging out in front of the firehouse.

It was pretty weird.

He'd sit on the wooden bench on the Quincy Street side of the firehouse, just to the right of the overhead door and all wrapped up in a gray woolen blanket. He didn't speak or otherwise engage anyone in normal, human communication. No eye contact, no nodding of the head. No nothing. He was just another Wolf Man sitting alone, enjoying the cool autumn evening. We gave Larry a wide berth preferring to observe him from two second floor windows situated in the front of the firehouse.

Without realizing it, just sitting there like a bump on that proverbial log, he provided us with hours of laughter. People would walk by, casually glance his way, do a quick double-take, look again, and run like hell! Some would scream!

"Ahhhhh! What the . . !"

Then Zooooooom!

Off they'd go as fast as their legs would carry them.

Larry didn't even have to move. All he had to do was sit there looking, well, looking as ugly as the Wolf Man he played in the 1941 movie.

It got to the point that people would bring other people around to have a look, but always from a very safe distance away. They would stand fifteen or twenty feet from the bench and prod Ol' Larry.

"Hey! Hey, you! Ugly ass!"

Larry wouldn't move - not even a little bit.

This little game went on for a few tours of duty. People came, yelled at Larry, and then left. He never reacted. It was all very strange. And he only appeared at night.

But one day - and we never figured out how this was allowed to happen - Larry somehow persuaded the Lieutenant to let him drive the fire engine to runs. Oh, and we were busy that day. We had ten or a dozen runs, or more - false alarms, car fires, but nothing serious. Larry drove very well. He knew where he was going; he knew the streets better than some of the guys who'd been there a while. Perhaps he'd been studying maps all the years he'd been cooped up in the nasty attic? I suppose he was.

Anyway, and of course, because it was broad daylight, everyone who saw Engine 24's pump drive by also saw Larry. He was hard to miss; big enough guy, a six-footer or so, average weight, maybe a buck sixty-five.

But, God, forgive me, he was ugly. He looked like … well, again, he looked exactly like the Wolf Man he played in the 1941 movie of the same name.

Ugly, hairy face.

Nasty skin.

He made people react.

Some screamed.

Some laughed.

Some were mesmerized but utterly speechless.

But Larry kept on driving.

On his last run of the day, as he passed by a woman standing on the street corner with her little son, two things happened: the woman screamed, the child cried. Not just sniffled and cried a few tears, but bellowed and screeched and bawled. The woman shook her fist at the passing fire engine.

It was good that it was the last run before the night crew arrived. Certainly the Lieutenant was second guessing himself all the way back to the firehouse and then, all the way back home. Would someone report Engine 24 to Headquarters? How could he explain allowing a Wolf Man to drive a genuine Boston fire engine back and forth to runs?

Fortunately, no one reported what they had seen driving the fire engine. The Lieutenant had skated. Engine 24 was off the hook.

Yup.

Nope.

Unknown to any of us, Larry had it in mind to sit out front one more time.

It happened on the next night tour, a cool, rainy

autumn evening. The kind of evening that keeps the nuisance running to a minimum. It was pretty quiet all over. Of course, it was still early and there was more than enough time to catch a fire or two or three before we went home the following morning. But for now, in the early evening, we just sort of hung out, waiting for the bells to ring.

Suddenly, there he was again.

Larry.

Gray blanket wrapped around him, sitting on the bench.

Motionless.

Owing to the cool weather and the rain, there weren't the usual number of people walking along Warren Street.

We watched from the second floor windows.

Soon, along came the coolest looking guy we'd seen in months. No, really, this guy was decked out like you read about. This was right about the time the movie Super Fly was popular and he was dressed to the nines ... huge Super Fly hat, platform shoes, leather pants.

He was diddy-boppin' along without a care in the world, lost inside the tunes playing in his head.

Then he saw Larry.

The Wolf Man.

Super Fly stopped dead in his tracks.

He stared.

Larry stared back.

Super Fly took a step closer.

He wasn't scared.

"Hey," he yelled.

Larry sat mute.

"Hey, brother," he tried again.

Nothing.

Super Fly was getting more curious and a little more brave.

The Wolf Man didn't move.

Super Fly stepped closer.

Then, in what had to be the bravest statement ever made to the Wolf Man or any of his kin, Super Fly took a step closer and said, "Man, if you ain't a statue, you are the ugliest motherfucker I ever did see."

That did it.

Larry leapt to his feet and stepping forward, threateningly raised his arms above his head and made a loud, guttural sound, something akin to "Aaargh!"

It was the fastest any of us had ever seen someone get off the line.

Super Fly was like a standing-still '72 Chevelle SS with a revved-up 454 that suddenly popped the clutch.

He took one step back and he was gone.

Poof!

Just like that.

Vanished.

Larry sat back down on the bench.

We laughed like hell from the safety of the second floor windows.

Less than five minutes later, we received a call from the Grove Hall firehouse, .9 miles away: "What the hell are you guys doing down there? We had a guy race in here, screaming that there was a monster in your front doorway." (Keep in mind that in 1972, the world record for the mile run was 3 minutes, 51.1 seconds, held by American Jim Ryun. Super Fly had come real close to covering that same distance - in platform shoes and leather pants - in near world record time.)

But it wasn't destined to go on. Nope. It just sort of stopped.

Within a year, they closed the fire house at 434 Warren Street.

Engine 24 was gone from the corner of Quincy and Warren.

It moved to Grove Hall to be with Ladder 23.

But the stories, tall tales, legends, yarns, and casts of characters associated with the Wolf Man events of the Summer of '72 live on.

No one ever saw Larry Talbot or the Wolf Man again. There were rumors handed down through the decades that he stayed in the attic and, in fact, still lives there.

Then there's another school of thought - one deserving of more careful study - that claims Larry Talbot never actually existed at all, that the Wolf Man was really a fireman, someone assigned to Engine 24, who was wearing a rubber mask.

I guess we'll never know for sure what really happened or who was involved, if anyone. But, I have to believe that if it were possible for us to enlist the support of the world's most famous consulting detective, after investigating the issues surrounding the strange events that took place inside and in front of that fire house, Mr. Sherlock Holmes would conclude: "It is an old maxim of mine that when you have excluded the impossible, whatever remains, however improbable, must be the truth."

SWASHBUCKLERS ALL

On September 2, 1949, Chief of Department, John F. McDonough, published an interesting Special Order. It stated that Dungarees were being distributed to the department and that they were to be worn by "privates" while on house watch. It also stated that the purpose of wearing these Dungarees was to save wear and tear on uniform trousers.

That the order prescribed Dungarees for house patrol to save uniform trousers but, at the same time, means that these same uniform trousers should still be worn at fires, is odd. It seems to me that if the city wanted to save the wear and tear on uniforms they should have told the guys to hang them in their lockers and use them only for ceremonial purposes. I mean, how much wear and tear was saved by not wearing them in the patrol desk?

However, by the time the war years rolled around in 1963, gone forever was the notion that wearing heavy woolen, often water-logged uniform trousers at a fire was a good idea. In their place (mercifully, I'm told) cotton Dungarees and chambray shirts, the kind of light weight, light blue shirts worn by U. S. Sailors, had become the uniform of the day for privates. Officers wore white shirts and regular uniform trousers or, later, a chino or "Dickies" type trouser. Not only were these new cotton uniforms better suited for fire duty, they were also a lot easier to care for. Unlike uniform trousers that needed to be dry-cleaned, a washing machine and some Duz or Oxydol was all firemen needed to keep themselves supplied in clean work clothes.

Long rubber coats with no liners were worn over the uniforms. They provided some protection from rain, snow, cold or inclement weather. They were cumbersome because they weren't very flexible; they tended to restrict your movement. In their place, different kinds of heavy cloth jackets began to appear. The jackets varied between what were properly called Naval Deck Coats (known more as US Navy foul weather jackets) - the heavy wool and alpaca-lined variety worn aboard ship by US sailors in WWII. Old army field jackets and Dungaree jackets were popular, too. Most jakes had two such jackets, lined and unlined. For obvious reasons, the unlined jacket was worn during warmer weather, the lined during cooler weather. In very cold weather, these cloth jackets would be worn under the long rubber coat. Talk about not being flexible!

Dungaree jackets were almost always blue although a

few brown ones could be seen from time to time. As the photographs verify, there were other options to the Dungaree jacket . . . like CYO bowling jackets, for instance. I once heard an opinion that so many different jackets made Boston's firemen look "like a band of pirates from Captain Blood," the old Errol Flynn swashbuckler movie. In short, it didn't seem to matter what the hell you wore. On the fire ground, it was not uncommon for firemen to go into buildings outfitted with Dungarees, a chambray shirt, and whatever jacket they chose to wear at any given time. Some wore gloves - but not everyone - and although everyone owned a pair of rubber boots, they weren't worn all the time. Most wore only black leather work shoes during the day and rubber boots only late at night. Sometimes they wore masks, sometimes they didn't. There weren't any hard and fast rules. It was left to the individual fireman's judgment about whether to wear a mask; a judgment that was based almost solely on how much smoke he could take. As you can imagine, some guys could suck up more smoke than others – some needed masks at every fire. As a result and over time, the amount of smoke a man could take became part of his identity. To be thought of as a bonafide "smoke eater" by your contemporaries was a badge of honor.

Things began to change however, when, on

November 23, 1967, Fire Lieutenant Warren Lynch died from smoke inhalation while working in the attic of a house in Roxbury. The incident was quickly investigated and it was determined that Lieutenant Lynch's death occurred when the All-Service gas mask he was wearing didn't provide him the protection it was supposed provide. They were ordered removed from all fire apparatus on January 15, 1968. In their stead, members were ordered to use cumbersome and seldom-used Chemox masks, self-contained monstrosities which were stored in large cases and tucked away in apparatus compartments. In fire house vernacular, these masks were a pain in the ass to use - they took too long to activate. It was easier to just leave the mask on the fire engine, then tuck your face inside your jacket and charge in the door with the line.

Earlier models of self-contained breathing apparatus (SCBA) - the air bottle type everyone uses today - were rushed into service after the All-Service was outlawed. Initially, these were also stored in large boxes and, so, weren't readily available. Eventually, as the apparatus began to change also - jump seats appeared in 1968 - the masks found their way into these jump seats where they could easily be placed for quick access. The internal SOP for engine companies was that the loop man would connect the feeder line to the pump, grab a mask, and head inside to back up the pipe man and the officer - the latter two always went inside first, without a mask. It seems archaic today, but keep in mind that the first effort was always aimed at putting quick water on the fire - masks could wait. Over the ensuing years the air masks were fine-tuned - and largely through the efforts of one man, Deputy Fire Chief, Leo Stapleton. In 1977, the final wooden stake was driven into the heart of the resistant smoke eaters when the department adopted the Mandatory Mask Rule.

It is an easy matter to look back and see that Lt. Lynch's death coincided with a rapid-fire change in department policy concerning safety and uniformity. It's not to say that the one event set the others in motion - it didn't. What we didn't know then was that the days of the pirate-like swashbucklers were drawing to a close.

About half-way through the war years, in October, 1972, a new work uniform was introduced. According to the general order, this was done "In an effort to improve the professional image of the Boston Fire Fighters and impress the general public of the professionalism of the fire service."

After a transition period between October and January, the old work uniform of Dungarees and chambray shirts would pass into history, to be replaced with navy blue work trousers without cuffs, black belts, navy blue work shirt (white shirt for officers), and black shoes. But the general order contained a very noticeable oddity. When the transition period ended on January 3rd, the new work uniform was required except, and I quote, "...when unusually dirty work is being performed in quarters." The irony escaped no one, save perhaps those who wrote the order. Unusually dirty work in quarters? What about unusually dirty work at fires?

The same general order included another change to the rules and regulations: henceforth, "Suitable and sufficient clothing to safeguard members against burns from direct flames, sparks, burning embers, heat, steam, and scalding water and against cold and inclement weather shall be worn while responding to and working at fires."

There was a likely a subtle connection between the two new orders. As almost everyone knows by now, all such navy blue work trousers were made of polyester materials. They had the tendency to melt when subjected to extreme heat - yup, the very kind of heat you may find in a burning building. This is pure conjecture on my part, but I'd find it very difficult to believe that the administration didn't know all about the dangers of wearing polyester clothing. That may be why they ordered that the now newly-uniformed firemen should wear their fire coats at all times and, so, to safeguard members against burns from direct flames, sparks, burning embers, heat, steam, and scalding water.

During the middle part of the war years - as new and younger officers were promoted to fill the ranks of the retiring members - the practice of requiring that officers wear white shirts both in the fire house and to fires came under closer scrutiny. Frankly, it was an old tradition that should have been done away with long ago.

I'm reminded that the possibility of changing the officers work shirts was posed to the Fire Commissioner at one of our Fire College meetings. The commissioner said that while he liked the white shirts best - they were symbols of authority. When someone reminded him that, first, everyone we worked with knew who we were and, second, that the first thing we did when we went on a run was to cover our symbol of authority with a fire coat or jacket he replied that he would entertain changing the shirts to, say, a shade of gray. One of our resident characters, a captain, "Big Al" to everyone who knew him, rose and replied, "Commissioner, all my white shirts are gray!" Even the commissioner had to laugh. Eventually, some years later, the department issued bark blue shirts and rank collar ornaments to their officers.

I've often wondered how some of the real swashbuckler old timers would react if they saw today's firemen walking around in shorts and T-shirts, waiting to jump into their bunker gear. I can hear them now: "Bunker gear? We didn't need no stinkin' bunker gear!"

Of all the different kinds of uniforms and safety items worn by Boston firemen through the years, though, the fire helmet is still the most personal. Different changes have been suggested from time to time but the overwhelming choice among the rank and file was then, and remains, the Cairns N5A New Yorker - leather, of course. Years of wear and tear and exposure to heat and smoke will affect the helmet and give it a salty look. The company numbers seen on the device affixed to the front of the helmet will get darker and darker as the wearer goes to more and more fires. As time goes by, each helmet takes on a personality of its own - it becomes a source of pride for the wearer because a well-worn helmet tends to indicate that it has seen a lot of service. However, that's not always the case. More than a limited number firemen have been known to wear helmets that have already been worn for many years - even some from outside Boston - so they'll look as salty as possible. Some like to change the shape of the helmet by bending the rear portion upward; the helmet is designed to shed water so, by necessity, it's formed so that it slopes down in back, away from the neck of the wearer. It is impossible for a leather helmet to turn up in the back as the result of normal, natural wear and tear. A common trick to this end was to place a wet helmet on a radiator so it would soften the leather and make it easier to bend. Another interesting habit was to use a well worn, out-of-town front piece - they're called "devices" in Boston - from a company with the same number as yours. They're worn instead of a regular Boston device, especially if yours is new and hasn't been at all darkened by exposure to fire and smoke.

HE GOT THE GIRL. NOW HE'S CLIMBING DOWN. CHECK OUT THE NIGHT HITCH HE'S WEARING.

THE JAKE ON THE RIGHT WILL MOVE THE 2 ½" LINE THROUGH THE WINDOW DRESSED AS YOU SEE HIM - NO FIRE COAT, BOOTS, OR GLOVES. JUST HIS HELMET AND DUNGAREE JACKET.

BUSY AS HELL

THE BOSS WOULD STAY DRESSED LIKE THAT DURING THE ENTIRE FIRE. NOTICE THE FEMALE COUPLINGS OF THE TWO LINES IN THE HOSE BEDS. THEY'RE NOT PRE-CONNECTED.

Two Ladder 4 jakes. Blue jacket, brown jacket. No one cared what you wore.

A Coincidental Sadness

A coincidence may be properly defined as "a remarkable concurrence of events or circumstances without apparent causal connection." For the two Fire Lieutenants who make up the subject matter in question, this definition is as accurate as it gets.

Perhaps a small disclaimer should be added here: this story is an intensely personal one for me because it deals with incidents in which I played a part and not in the way one appreciates or looks back upon with any measure of happiness.

You see, on Friday, February 2, 1968, my brother, PFC Robert P. Foley was killed in action in Vietnam and to make a dreadful situation even worse - if such is even possible - he died on his 19th birthday.

Bobby was a United States Marine, serving with M Company, 1st Battalion, 3rd Marines, 1st Marine Division. He was killed outright, gunned down by an automatic weapon as he crossed a rice paddy while his company was in pursuit of fleeing remnants of the 318th battalion of the North Vietnamese Army (NVA). His body was recovered immediately.

On the very same day, another young Bostonian was

killed in action in Vietnam. His name was Sp4 George J. Gottwald, Jr.; he served with 2nd Battalion, 16th Infantry, 1st Infantry Division. In heart wrenching and situational contrast, young Gottwald died with several other soldiers when his unit was overrun by the Viet Cong during a bitter engagement around An My, about 4 kilometers northwest of the Phu Loi airfield. Owing to the nature of the conflict itself - his unit's position was abandoned - and Sp4 Gottwald was listed as Missing in Action until his remains could be recovered, some twelve days later.

Both young men were sons of Fire Lieutenants assigned to adjacent firehouses in District 7: Lt. Robert P. Foley was assigned to Ladder 7 on Meeting House Hill while Lt. George Gottwald was assigned to the Rescue-Pumper Unit in Grove Hall.

I remember the first time I met Lieutenant George Gottwald. It was at my brother's wake in Mulry's Funeral Home on Dorchester Avenue, right around the corner from the house I lived in on Whitten Street. George had arrived to pay his respects to my father - who he knew very well - and the rest of our family. It was during this first meeting that George told my father and I that the army had just notified him that his son's remains had been recovered; his status was changed from Missing in Action to Killed in Action. Whatever hope the Gottwald family had held out for the safety and well being of their son and brother over the ensuing almost two weeks was yanked from them in a simple but cruel exchange of letters - change the M in MIA to a K in KIA and there it is. He's dead. That's it. The date of his death was determined to have been February 2, 1968. I suspect that you would be inclined to believe that this would be coincidence enough for a lifetime, right? Well, it gets even more weird.

Fast forward almost two years - to Tuesday, January 27, 1970, a bitterly cold night; the temperature was hovering in the single digits and there was a medium to strong wind blowing in off the nearby ocean where the Neponset River empties into the south western portion of Boston harbor.

At 1:24 AM, Ladder 7 responded from Meeting House Hill to 220 Victory Road, the location of a 110-foot high gas tank belonging to the Boston Gas Company. At about the same time, the Rescue Pumper Unit (RPU) was dispatched to Victory Road from its quarters in Grove Hall, about twice the distance away from Victory Road.

When Ladder 7 arrived, they were informed that a man had illegally entered the gas company property and then managed to climb a long steel ladder to the top of the tank's sidewall before moving to another ladder that took him to the top where he now sat.

The man was threatening to jump.

The top of the tank was beyond the reach of Ladder 7's aerial ladder so the Lieutenant took a single firefighter with him and followed the man's path upward, making their way along the icy stairs on the exterior ladder that followed the contour of the cylindrical tank as it ascended. Reaching the top of the stairs, they then moved to the next ladder, a laid-flat ladder that was secured to the top of the tank and which lead to the absolute top of the tank where the man was seated.

A few minutes later, the Rescue Pumper Unit arrived and after being informed of the situation, the Lieutenant took one firefighter with him and mirrored Ladder 7's approach by ascending to the top of the tank on the opposite side. When they reached the tippity-top, the members of Ladder 7 were already there. They learned that the jumper was a just-returned veteran of the Vietnam war. He was distraught and wanting to end his life.

Can you picture the scene?

Two Lieutenants who lost sons on the very same day almost two years previous perched atop a 100-foot tall tank shielding themselves and the veteran from the biting wind and bitter cold trying to tell him not to jump - that death wasn't the answer.

Did they talk about their own sons?

I assume they did.

Yes, of course they did.

But, what did they say?

Did they remind the veteran that for whatever reason, and unlike their sons, God had spared his life?

Was the jumper the same age as their sons had been?

Did he remind them of their sons?

Did they see the faces of their own dead sons in their minds eye's and decide that maybe, just maybe, a quick and virtually painless death by massed gunfire in a jungle 10,000 miles away was somehow preferable to the torment this veteran was enduring?

Did they think about any of this?

Did they fight back tears as they talked?

Did they take a tough love tactic with the veteran and chastise him for even considering suicide?

Did they remind him that there were now five men on that tank, any one of whom could have slipped and fallen 100-feet to their death?

All because of him climbing up there in the first place?

Or did they handle him with kid gloves, speaking in measured tones?

Did they come close to begging him not to jump?

Well, whatever they said, however they said it, worked.

The distraught veteran decided not to jump.

With some help from the others, Ladder 7's Lieutenant took the veteran over his shoulder and carried the reconciled man half way down the external ladder, toward the ground. About halfway down, the Lieutenant, exhausted and unable to go on, transferred the man to the shoulder of the Ladder 7 firefighter for the rest of the trip.

The incident over; the four men climbed back about their respective fire engines and went back to their firehouses.

But the two Lieutenants had more terrible irony to consider.

Remember that both had lost sons in Vietnam on February 2, 1968. Remember that February 2nd was PFC Foley's 19th birthday.

Then factor this into the equation ….

January 27th, the date the two Lieutenants talked the veteran down off that gas tank …. that was the now deceased Sp4 George J. Gottwald, Jr's 22nd birthday.

Extra Special Lunch

If asked to share their opinion, the average person would probably say that fireman, having seen all manner of grisly scenes during their careers, have pretty strong stomachs. Normally, they'd be correct. But there was a rumor circulating through a certain fire house, one suggesting that the Captain, a grizzled veteran of over thirty years, a man who's very first run as a brand new fireman was on November 28, 1942, to the Cocoanut Grove fire, had a very weak stomach and would (as they say) lose his lunch at the slightest appearance of blood or similar calamity.

So, given the rumors, meet our chief antagonist as he sets out to prove the rumor true - or, maybe, false.

For any rumor-busting plan to work, it had to be stealth, below the radar. It had to be delivered at a time and place where the marked Captain would have no warning that anything was amiss. For verification purposes, it had to be carried out when as many firemen as possible would be present to witness the result. In other words, it would take some careful planning and perfect execution.

After a brief analysis, the perpetrator had it figured out. He knew what to do. He told three or four firemen about his plan. They all laughed like hell and wondered whether it would really work. The perp, the very soul of self confidence, assured them it would.

The fire house kitchen was the theater.

The kitchen table was the stage.

So, one day at precisely 1145 hours, as was his habit, the Captain walked into the kitchen, sat down and began eating his lunch.

The perp walked in right behind him and sat across the table. He made some small talk for a minute with three or four other firemen seated nearby and then, on cue, announced that watching the Captain eat his lunch was making him hungry.

So, he casually walked a few steps across the small kitchen and removed a bowl from the shelf above the kitchen sink. He then took a tablespoon from the drawer, removed a quart of milk from the refrigerator and placed the items on the table across from the Captain. So far, everything looked normal. The Captain had no reason to assume anything was wrong.

Then the perp delivered the coup de grâce.

Remember those shiny silver cardboard ashtrays that you'd see on the tables at functions? They were about three inches square, with four indentations on each corner to rest cigarettes. Well, firehouses sometimes used them in their pest control efforts. They'd put them in corners of different rooms and fill them with rat poison that looks a lot like oatmeal.

See the plot yet?

Our perp took a few steps toward the corner of the kitchen, to a place just below the back window and near the radiator. He reached down, picked up the silver ashtray, walked back to the table and dumped the contents into the bowl. As the Captain watched, the perp sat down, poured some milk in the bowl, spooned out a big bite and put it in his mouth. The Captain was ashen. Perp smiled and said, "You know, Cap, this shit isn't really that bad."

The Captain gasped for air, slumped forward onto the table top and promptly passed out. Boom!

So there it was.

The rumors were true.

Not only did the Captain have a weak stomach, he had no stomach. None.

But our story doesn't end there, no sir.

You see, having done his research, the diabolical Mr. Perpetrator anticipated what would happen next.

As the witnesses went to the Captain's aid, he started to come to. Shaken, he was still ashen white and quite clearly not feeling very well. He was too defeated to care (or wonder) whether he'd been pranked or whether the perp was, in fact, certifiable.

He got up slowly and headed for the stairway that led to the second floor where his office was situated. He'd have been okay if he didn't stop in the small bathroom on the main apparatus floor.

But he did stop.

And so, unleashed Phase II.

The perp, and one of his equally sinister compatriots, had squirted ketchup all over the walls and toilet, which, to someone with a weak stomach, someone who'd just seen one of his guys eat rat poison, looked exactly like blood. The Captain stumbled out of the bathroom, groaning loudly and more ashen than before. He somehow managed to keep his feet long enough to climb the stairs and walk down the long corridor to his office.

Of course, Ol' Perp wasn't that stupid. You have probably assumed that he had removed the ashtray filled with rat poison long before the Captain arrived and replaced it with one filled with real Quaker oatmeal. And you would be right.

Here comes Santa Claus ... Hey, Not So Fast

A so-called paid detail occurs when a public fire department provides a measure of fire protection or presence to a private concern on an individual contract basis. According to the BFD's web site, a paid detail is required for issuance of the permit for an event or work to be performed or if there is a life safety condition in the building such as a disabled fire alarm or sprinkler system and the district chief requires it as a condition of the building remaining occupied throughout the duration of inoperability to protect life and property.

Years ago, paid details were few and far between for most companies. It used to be that the details were kept in the district where the private business was located. For example, Engine 4 and Ladder 24, two companies in the then detail rich District 3, helped supply the fire protection for the old Jordan Marsh company at Christmas time.

It was called the "Santa Claus detail," even though it had nothing to do with Santa Claus himself. It was, rather, a detailed fireman's job to keep an eye on the area on the 6th floor where the company set out a huge

Christmas display called The Enchanted Village; a display that was originally created in 1958. At that time, Jordan Marsh Company commissioned a Bavarian toy maker to create 28 fully decorated holiday scenes with 250 magically animated figures. Throughout the 1960s and into the 1970s, Jordan Marsh displayed the Enchanted Village in its Downtown Crossing store. The heart-warming display quickly became an integral part of New England's seasonal celebrations. Until 1972, when Jordan Marsh closed the display, a trip to The Village was a traditional event.

Well, one year the Captain of Engine 4 asked a new, young fireman whether he wanted the Santa Claus detail. He added that it paid $28 for four hours work. Now, for a guy making $134 per week, $28 is a lot of money. So, naturally, the new guy said yes, he would love to work the extra hours. The Captain told him where to report and when, and to arrive at least fifteen minutes before the start of his shift. The young fireman smiled broadly and said, yes, he would be happy to do whatever it took to make a good impression.

Fast forward a few days.

The young fireman is excited as he rides the subway to Washington Street station - in 1985, the name was changed to Downtown Crossing - takes the escalator to Summer Street, locates the Jordan Marsh building and takes the elevator to the 6th floor.

BUSY AS HELL

Filled with youthful exuberance and a desire to please the Captain, the young fireman found the office where he had been instructed to report. Good, he thought, I'm twenty minutes early. As he entered the office, he saw a secretary sitting behind a desk. He told her that he was from the fire department and was there for the Santa Claus detail.

The secretary looked at him, nodded, and said she'd be right back. Very shortly, a man came out of an office and spoke to the young fireman.

"You're from the fire department?"

"Yes," he replied, beaming.

"You're here for the Santa Claus detail?"

"Why are you wearing civilian clothes?"

"I don't understand."

"If you're here from the fire department, where's your uniform?"

"Uniform?"

"Yes, your uniform. Why aren't you wearing it?"

"Look buddy, I don't know what the hell this is all about, but if you want me to play Santa Claus, you're gonna have to loan me a red and white suit 'cause I don't have one of my own."

Shutting The Doors - Firing The Help

1981 started out poorly.

On January 6, two firemen, Lt. Paul Lentini and Jimmy Gibbons, both of Engine 37, were killed when the upper floors of the building at 16-17 Arlington Street, Back Bay, collapsed. Many members were trapped inside the rubble. It would take hours to extricate everyone. The rescue efforts labored on through the night and finally concluded with all but two members surviving. While 1981 never got any worse than losing two good guys, it never got any better, either.

It all began in April . . . politicians met in their proverbial "smoke-filled back rooms" and used firemen, cops, and other city workers as pawns in their political chess match centered on what they generally perceived as the lack of revenue. At issue was the recent passage of a property tax limiting referendum that had appeared on the state-wide ballot in 1980 when the electorate told the politicians that they were tired of high property taxes and, so, adopted what is known as "Prop 2 ½." Briefly, the new law said that the ability to assess property taxes in cities and towns was capped at 2.5% of their entire assessed property value and further, that the annual increase in the city or town's property tax assessment was also capped at 2.5%. In Massachusetts, one of the bluest of the blue states, this simply wasn't the way things were supposed to be. Citizens weren't supposed to be able to partially take their government back, take it firmly by the throat and shake it until the spendthrift politicos stopped. But they did.

Much has been written about the political machinations and posturing that went on behind closed doors and in front of TV cameras. The state blamed the city; the city blamed the state; the state supported one solution, the city supported another. The furor intensified, the name calling grew louder, and blame game dragged on and on for almost a year.

This writer has nothing of value to add to the political side of the discussion, so I'll stop right here - but only after reminding everyone that for all the bravado and, yes, bullshit, there are a few things that the politicians never did or even suggested:

They never introduced a bill to reduce or suspend their own salaries and per diem, never displayed an interest in reducing the size of the legislature or of laying off or firing any of their personal staff, they never did anything but wring their hands and publicly bemoan the loss of firemen, cops and other city workers.

When the dust settled eleven months later, the department had been sliced and diced, a shadow of its former self.

Gone forever were District 2 and 13, engine companies 1, 11, 12, 25, 26, 34, 36, 40, 43, 45 and ladder companies 5, 8, 13, 20, 22, 30, and AT2. Disbanded but returned to service were engine 49, 50 and 54, Ladder 31, and Rescue 2. Half-a-handful of companies were moved to other locations or returned to service in consolidated form.

Over 200 members took a one-time cash incentive and retired before they'd originally planned to do so, taking over 8000 years of experience with them as most had been hired in the late 1940s. Hundreds of firemen had been laid off, scores were demoted. Yes, it's true, most were re-hired and restored to their original rank but not without severe fallout. While some unconcerned with-details people would consider such things as minor inconveniences, those affected would report different results.

Laid-off firemen were advised that they could collect unemployment. "Oh, goody. Let me try and survive with a 60% pay cut. The kids aren't really that hungry, the bank will understand, right?"

For demoted officers . . . well, when you're a Captain, you receive Captain's pay. Every week, the check comes; every week you're paid as a captain. But when you're demoted, you're a Lieutenant again . . . a mere acting Captain. The dollars are the same but the method of payment is different. Every single demoted member had to fill out "acting papers" at the end of the month and wait to receive the difference in salary. Small potatoes? Maybe. Maybe not. If you're on a budget, like most are, the lack of funds on a regular, predicable basis can be troublesome. What about paying the bills in a timely manner? What happens to that theory if you suddenly take a 15% cut in pay and for doing the same job, too? Again, the money is paid eventually but it just isn't the same. Lenders weren't exactly lining up to accept partial payments, late payments, or no payments. Payments march on.

There's no way to measure the unseen damage the layoffs caused. I know for certain that homes were lost and families were severely tested. Some weathered the storm, some did not. There had to be a number of layoff-related divorces.

Yet, for all the furor and needless political pandering, Boston's firemen stood tall.

We still showed up every time someone called us.

We still put out their fires and got their cats out of trees.

We did our job.

And that's no bullshit.

The Quintessential Straight Man

We worked with a District Fire Chief, a tall, rather slim man who always reminded me of Basil Rathbone. He was a man of few words. The fewer the better, in fact. But the words he chose to utter were smart and clever, like a Stiletto slipped right into the funny bone. He could have been a straight man for any comedic genius, anywhere, anytime.

When he was in District 9, one of the firefighters on Engine 42 was rewarded for (rightfully) escaping a nasty civilian issue when his case was dismissed for, not just lack of, but the absence of any evidence against him.

So, to celebrate the event, the mother of this fire fighter sent a singing telegram to the fire house, which turned out to be a young college student dressed as a bumble bee. That's right, a bumble bee - complete with a black body suit, antenna on his head, and yellow stripes and everything.

Anyway, Bumble Bee Kid went into his song and dance routine which seemed interminably long at a minute or so. We all felt for the poor kid who certainly felt pretty stupid while emphasizing what lengths students would go to earn a buck. Finally, the little routine was over and we all applauded. The kid was thankful and said that we weren't as tough an audience as he had suspected.

The chief, standing next to the coffee pot and soaking all of this in, finally got Bumble Bee Kid's attention and in his soft, laconic style, asked: "You want a cup of coffee? Glass of honey? We have honey."

Another time, at night, we had a fire in a large, three story, wooden duplex building sitting prominently at the end of a dead end street. Usually, this sized building housed six families although in this instance, one or two apartments may have been vacant.

Upon arrival, the chief made his initial report: he had fire on two floors. We still hadn't arrived at the scene but our plan was to bring a couple of hundred feet of 2½-inch hose with us when we reported to him at the front of the building. This was a common occurrence. Instead of running up and asking the chief what he wants, we would anticipate; we'd assume he would want us to run a line into the building, so, we'd bring it with us and then just ask where he wanted it. (Our old-time officers taught us well. "If he has a good fire, there isn't a chief alive that'll chastise you for bringing a line with you, looking for a place to use it," they'd say.)

So, here we are, trooping up the street dragging a big line behind us. I was not prepared for what greeted us. The boss was sitting on the hood of his car, sans a fire coat and helmet. He had his feet up on the front bumper, his elbows were resting on his knees and was smoking a cigarette. He couldn't have seemed more unconcerned. He looked more like a spectator than the man in charge.

When we arrived with the line of hose, with a smile, I said: "Engine 42 with a big line. What's your pleasure, boss?"

With a bigger smile: "My pleasure, Michael, would be for you to put the fire out," he said as he thumb-motioned toward the building like he was hitchhiking. "But be careful, better use your masks. You smell that shit?" he added.

I laughed out loud. "Well, yes, actually we do smell that shit."

He laughed and took a drag off his cigarette.

"Have fun. But not too much," he smirked as we trudged off toward the stairs.

It was a local drug house.

The place was filled with marijuana.

And so, too, was the air.

You could smell it for blocks away.

It was the largest crowd of spectators we'd seen in a long time.

On another morning, over coffee, the chief told a story about going to a travel agent with his wife and telling the agent that they wanted to vacation in a secluded, beach-type hotel in the tropics.

"I told them I wanted to see as few other vacationers as possible. If I wanted to mingle," he added, "I'd stay in the firehouse kitchen for two weeks. Nope, I want to go where no one else goes. I wanted to be as alone as possible."

The travel agent said she understood and showed them brochures for exotic, off-the-beaten-path resorts. After a brief discussion, they settled on a location.

"I was pretty pumped," he said, "I just wanted two weeks away from the world. Just me and my wife. Quiet dinners, couple of cocktails, and a time to rest quietly. I'm thinking it's going to be like heaven."

"How did everything go," someone asked.

"Terrible!" he exclaimed.

"Huh?"

"The first day we're there, I'm sitting in a lounge chair on the beach. Kicked back. Relaxin'. The place is deserted, not another soul for miles. I'm thinking this is pretty good. Then, way off in the distance, I see a couple approaching. One other couple. So it's just us and them. What could go wrong? I asked myself."

"What happened?"

"The couple is walking up the beach, toward me, getting closer, but I'm paying less and less attention. I sit back on the lounge chair and close my eyes, catching some rays. Then suddenly I hear, 'Hey, Chief! What the hell are you doing here?' I opened my eyes and find myself staring into the face of a Lieutenant from Ladder 17. Worst goddamned vacation of my life."

RIP, Leo.

Conscientiousness On Steroids

The brand new Captain was a nice guy, a humble, faithful, and decent man. He was personable and happy. He laughed a lot. He watched Dark Shadows every afternoon, laughing like hell at the antics of its chief protagonist, Barnabas Collins. Typical of most mid-50s men, he took no small measure of delight in cheating on his diet when he was in the fire house. More than once, one of the firemen walked into the kitchen just when he was bent over with his head stuck in the refrigerator, looking for something to munch on. Caught red handed, the Captain would react the way a child might if he'd been found with his hand in the proverbial cookie jar. He'd giggle and make believe he was doing something, anything, more than foraging for leftovers. In short, he was an absolute delight.

But he was also terribly miscast. In addition to having worked in a neighboring town's fire department for eight years, he'd been working in quieter, home-guard ladder companies in East Boston for going on twenty-five years. He had no real sense for the amount of work we were doing on the Boston side of the tunnel. Sure, he heard many of our fires over the radio but that was pretty much it. Yet, with his over thirty years of service and experience, I'm certain he thought he knew and understood what awaited him when he was promoted and transferred to Engine 24 in mid-September, 1969.

The first sign of the sadness and severity of the miscast appeared during one of his first tours of duty when he walked to work. Now, on the surface, this single act seems pretty innocuous. It's only about .9 miles from where the Captain lived to where he worked at 434 Warren Street. The first two or three times he came to work, he drove his car. It took all of three or four minutes, and along the way he probably didn't notice much difference. The kids were back in school and there wasn't a lot of street activity. In fact, he felt safe enough to have his wife drive him once or twice.

But one day he decided to walk - a whole different thing. That .9 miles may just as well have been 20 miles, or 100 miles, because he had to cross Columbia Road - the unofficial yet fairly obvious boundary line separating two very different neighborhoods, i. e., the white neighborhood and the black neighborhood.

Keep in mind that things were very different then, in the 60s. In 1965, the so-called Watts race riots had exploded in Los Angeles. 1966 through 1969 would see more race riots nationwide, over a dozen. Boston experienced its own race riot just two years earlier, in June 1967, during what came to be known nationally as the Long Hot Summer. Tensions remained high. Racial attacks on red fire engines and white firemen were common. Often, while you drove to the fire house, a palpable tension accompanied you. It was eerie. And scary. One event sits prominently in my memory, not for the results of the incident but for the planning that went into its execution. Engine 24 responded to box 2181, which turned out to be a false alarm. We approached the location from the Elm Hill Avenue end of Homestead Street and rolled up to the intersection at Humboldt Avenue. Then, just as the Lieutenant reported that there was nothing showing, we were bombarded by large rocks from a roof top to our right. The two of us riding in the jump seats dove for cover under the roof. The driver sized up the situation instantly, jammed the accelerator to the floor, and turned right, heading down Humboldt Avenue. At the same instant, about ten kids jumped up from behind a row of hedges directly to our front and continued the attack. It was a perfectly executed linear ambush. Any combat unit would have been proud to execute one as well. Fortunately, save a few dents, we escaped unscathed.

It was under these conditions and tensions that the Captain embarked upon what had to be a most frightening journey. When he arrived at the fire house after walking from home, he was visibly shaken. He sat nervously in the kitchen trying to collect himself. He said he felt as if every eye followed him while he walked along the sidewalk; they were not friendly eyes, he added. As he further explained the ten minute walk, there was not an ounce of bravado in his voice. Despite his role as company commander, everyone's boss, there was no attempt to pooh-pooh the obvious. He'd been scared to death and admitted as much. It was as though he'd lost his innocence. To their eternal credit, and to a man, the members rallied around their Captain. Yes, he exactly didn't exactly fit the image of what they wanted or expected in a company commander but, dammit, he was their company commander. From that moment on, they more or less took him under their wing and protected him. They accepted his borderline haplessness and made the best of a difficult situation.

While the Captain did his best to fit in, he wasn't up to the task in an overall sense. He was efficient in his office-like duties but seemed like the proverbial duck out of water when it came to the fire duty. More than once, he was left standing alone in the doorway or on the sidewalk, pondering his next move while the younger fire fighters forced the line inside to attack the fire. The young guys were full of piss and vinegar; the old Captain was content to attack the fire from the outside or at least spend more time sizing up the situation. The two theories didn't blend well and it soon became common thinking that Engine 24 had lost some of its aggressiveness when the Captain was working - an unthinkable assessment to firemen who took pride in their ability to match speed, effort, and overall effectiveness with all their swashbuckling brethren. As a result, the firemen over compensated and the situation got worse - they charged ahead at every opportunity to prove their worth while the Captain hung back and, so, became more and more irrelevant.

He didn't help himself very much by bringing a rather overbearing sense of conscientiousness along with him from East Boston. In other words, he nitpicked with the best of them. Before very long, he earned the nickname Colonel Klink - one only needs to see one episode of Hogan's Heroes to see the similarities between the Captain and the TV character.

One day he put a notice on the bulletin board demanding the immediate return of two acid carboys that had disappeared from the cellar. This was tantamount to demanding the return of a horse bridle that had hung on a hook in the same cellar for almost 50 years after Engine 24 received its first motorized fire engine and, so, sent the horses to the glue factory. The problem with the acid carboys was that they'd disappeared years before he arrived. But, dammit, they were on his inventory list and he was going to account for them.

The poor guy became the butt of many practical jokes. It was sad to watch. When we received a new Hahn pump in 1970, the Captain treated it like a museum piece. Naturally, the other officers and almost all the fire fighters took very good care of the apparatus, too, but everyone also realized the inevitable - dings and dents would appear; regular wear and tear couldn't be helped. We were very busy and went to a lot of fires. Things were bound to happen. But we tried to keep ahead of the curve by washing the fire engine every day. Some of us even polished it. One of the guys added extra red lights to make ourselves more visible. All in all it was a terrific pump; it purred like a kitten and gave us all the water we needed, and it was fast as hell.

But the Captain's penchant for inspecting the fire engine with a fine tooth comb every tour of duty played right into the hands of the jokers. One day, just for kicks, someone took two or three little bolts and a few nuts and tossed them on the floor under the piece then sat back and waited for the fireworks. Sure enough here came the Captain looking around here and there, touching tiny new dings as if he was inspecting a used car on a car lot.

Then he saw them.

The bolts and nuts on the floor.

As they say, you had to be there. He went crazy!

He raced around to his side of the front seat and removed his big, officer's wheat light. Then he almost ran to a little space between a hose rack and the wall where the creeper was kept. He dragged the creeper across the floor and positioned it right beside the apparatus. Then, with some difficulty - remember, he was in his mid 50s - he laid down on the creeper and using his feet like pistons against the concrete pushed himself underneath. He collected the bolts and nuts and for the next thirty or forty minutes he pushed himself from side to side and from one end of the fire engine to the other and then back again shining his light and looking for the holes in the frame where bolts may have come from. Finally, satisfied that there was nothing amiss, he came out from under the fire engine and went back about his business. He never said anything, but I imagine he figured it out later on.

It was impossible not to the love the guy, but everyone understood that while, yes, he was a bit of an old lady in the fire house, his personality trumped the nitpicking. It was his reaction when the bells rang, and we had work to do that was tough to take.

But while I sat here and wrote this - while my sense of propriety overcame me and blurred out the less than happy parts - one enduring image of the Captain forced its way to the forefront.

His smile was radiant.

His laugh was infectious.

He had a good heart and he left us too soon.

Rest in peace, Cap.

BUSY AS HELL

SAFE CRACKERS

Ever see that TV show, America's Dumbest Criminals? It always cracks me up. How can they be so stupid? My favorite is the one about the guy who robs a girl and makes his escape. The victim describes the perp to the cops who find him in about five minutes. They tell him they need him for ID purposes so they bring him back to the scene of the crime. He gets out of the car, looks at the woman he just robbed and says, "Yeah, that's her."

Well, too bad they didn't have that show back in the early 70s because the knuckleheads who tried to rob a bank in the middle of the night with dynamite would have won first prize for Dumbest of the Year.

Seems that the Jesse James Gang wannabes decided they'd put some dynamite in front of the safe on the second floor, light the fuse, stand back a little, watch it blow up, then reach inside the safe, grab the loot and beat it.

Well, that's almost how it happened.

Instead, someone called the fire department because of the fire.

Engine 52 and Ladder 29 roared the few blocks

down Blue Hill Avenue and had to do a double take when they arrived.

What was this in the street?

Well, for starters, the front of the building was.

Secondly, the safe.

Thirdly, the bank robbers.

I think one of them lived at least long enough to tell his side of the story. Sort of like The Sundance Kid to Butch Cassidy when they blew the door of the Union Pacific railroad car: "Think we used enough dynamite there, Butch?"

Pranks

Fire fighting enjoys a well-suited and common comparison with the wartime military. There's often a lot of waiting around for something to happen and then here it comes, spurts of furious, high intensity and in some cases, semi-violent activity. It's not the same as a full-fledged war, of course, but it is like the aforementioned series of barroom brawls.

As if by design, the men who served these roles and lived through these times developed a strong understanding of gallows humor and then, after much practice, fine tuned it and eventually turned it into an art form.

Wikipedia, the free online encyclopedia, defines gallows humor as being a form of "witticism in the face of - and in response to a hopeless situation. It arises from stressful, traumatic, or life-threatening situations."

It is against this backdrop that firemen developed their sense of humor and took them to different, more sophisticated levels. Consider the following pranks and their most frequent ingredients.

WATER

One morning, just before shift change, Eddie decided it would be a real good idea to hide inside the-soon-to-arrive Jack's locker with a fire extinguisher and then, when Jack opened his locker to get his fire gear, to douse him from head to toe. When the appointed day arrived, cramped but happy to endure the tightness inside the locker if it bore fruit, Eddie waited for Jack to open the door.

Well, right on cue, Jack arrived in the fire house, immediately went to his locker and opened the door. Eddie got him and got him good. Real good. Jack, a prankster in his own right, was surprised and couldn't decide which was better, closing the door or jumping back and away from the stream of water. In the split second it took his brain to decide, Eddie had squirted enough water from the extinguisher to drench Jack pretty much all over. Eddie laughed evilly and Jack, always the good sport, laughed right along with him though vowing to get him back. It was at this very instant that Jack began plotting his revenge.

The old saying, "revenge is a dish best served cold," was not lost on Jack. He took his sweet time planning to return the favor because he understood that the payback would need to be something Eddie couldn't anticipate and therefore, plan to avoid. It had to completely unexpected. In all, it probably didn't take Jack very long to figure things out. He just needed some time for Eddie to relax his guard a bit before he struck.

Finally, the day arrived. Jack came to work extra early and seeking to capitalize on Eddie's fine effort, he planned to also use water.

But not from a fire extinguisher.

No, sir. A measly little extinguisher wasn't good enough for Jack. No, this was different. Jack needed to make a statement.

So what does he do? Well, he removed 200-feet of 1½-inch line from the fire engine, hooked it up to the hydrant in front of the fire house, opened the hydrant thus filling the hose with water, dragged it through the door, up the stairs, down the hall and into the bunk room where, you guessed it, Eddie was sound asleep. One can only imagine the amazing sense of utter victory coursing through Jack's veins as he pulled the handle on the nozzle back and woke Eddie - tsunamied him off the bed and on to the floor with what had to be a million times more water than some chintzy little fire extinguisher.

When it came to filling a fire house with laughter, Jack had no superior. I remember being detailed to Ladder 29 one night and seeing him walking around in a long night shirt and cap, carrying a candle, just like you might picture them doing in The Night Before Christmas.

But odd dress aside, as Eddie learned and learned well, when it came to pranks Jack was not a man to be trifled with.

MORE WATER

One of the Engine 13 firemen was a slow moving kind of guy. He was never in a hurry to do anything; no sense of urgency ever entered his blood stream. As such, he was an easy target for faster moving, more industrious - shall we say, mischievous types.

One hot summer day, one of the perennial trouble makers decided to throw water on the Slow Mover. The ploy worked and a good laugh was had by all. Well, it was so much fun that the instigator did it again. Only this time he used more water, about a cup full:

Splash!

Ha! Ha! Ha!

Okay, Slow Mover thought, that does it! I'll get him back. So off he goes searching for a proper-sized receptacle in which to carry enough water to get the revenge job done.

Finally, after a time, there it is, Slow Mover thought,

a bucket! I'll fill this sucker up to the top and drench that little wise ass.

So, off he goes to the side of the fire house where he finds a faucet and fills the bucket. Of course, the instigator was watching and just when Slow Mover thought he was alone in his thinking, the former emptied another glass of water on the latter.

Surprisingly, Slow Mover grabbed the bucket filled with water and started running, actually running after the instigator. Around the main apparatus floor they ran, the former chasing the latter.

Just then, the Instigator broke away and escaped out through the wide-open front doors. The Slow Mover gave chase and followed him out the door. Instantly, as he turned to his right, Slow Mover saw the instigator sitting down on the bench and let heave the contents of the bucket. Only then did Slow Mover see that the instigator had sat down directly beside the Captain, a less than humorous kind of guy. The actions that took place in the next milliseconds have since been reported upon no less than a million times in the ensuing years: Slow Mover, complete with the requisite horrified look upon his face, dropping the bucket and trying for all he was worth to reach out, collect the water, and bring it back into the bucket.

To the Captain's everlasting credit, he got up without saying a word, went upstairs and changed his uniform.

FURNITURE

One of the firemen who drove one of the areas engine companies was pretty short. If I had to guess, I'd say he was no more than 5-feet, 5-inches tall and, like many his size, had a severe case of what we all call the "Napoleon Complex." In another profession he may have been less likely to feel that his lack of altitudinal stature was a detriment. But here, in the often macho, rough and tumble world of fire fighting, it didn't help his feelings of self worth to be shorter than everyone else. For instance, the fire coats we wore hung down a little lower on his body which only added to the impression that he was wearing one ten sizes too big or, shudder, that he was standing in a hole. Now many similarly height-challenged firemen tackled their stature issues by studying hard and getting promoted - some as many as four times. Not this guy. Oh, he tried studying but never seemed able to crack the books enough - or get lucky enough on exam day - to get promoted once and make Lieutenant. These fruitless attempts only made him more disagreeable and twice as ornery. Heaven help the fireman who had less time on the job than him but had the audacity to get promoted before he did. It was a ticket to his personal Hall of Hate, a feeling he did little if anything to conceal. Translation: he was a disagreeable guy, a royal pain in the ass.

So, then, if you've been following our story so far, you know that this unnamed fireman was also ripe for target practice and, further, that there were certain guys who waited for the perfect occasion to give him something to really bitch about. As luck would have it, the opportunity presented itself at a rubbish fire one day when one of the guys noticed a certain discarded item laying on the ground near a dumpster.

He picked it up and tossed it into the jump seat of the ladder truck, and when he got back to the fire house he hid it in his locker until the proper moment which, as it turned out, was several weeks later.

Anyway, finally, the short fireman came to work for the night shift, and because he was driving he checked the pump to make sure everything was copacetic; he made sure the booster tank was filled, checked the hose pre-connections, started the pump and put it in pump gear. In short, he did all the things a good driver does to get ready for the tour. Satisfied that everything was okay, he put his gear in the front seat and on the floor and closed the door. The next time he would see the inside of the fire engine was when they had a run.

From the shadows, our perpetrator emerged. He slipped unnoticed across the floor, opened the fire engine door, placed something on the driver's seat and quietly closed the door. All they had to do now was wait for the house gong to go off.

As if they needed any more reason to enjoy pranking the driver, he was in the kitchen being a lot more obnoxious than usual. He was on a roll ... this sucked, that sucked, this new, young Lieutenant is an asshole, blah, blah, blah.

All of a sudden, Fire Alarm hopped to the rescue.

The engine had a run and they were going out alone!

This meant that the laddermen who would be staying behind could watch the prank unfold without interruption. This was perfect! - they thought.

So, the short fireman, a bit immersed in his own self-importance (as usual) walked quickly to the door of the fire engine and opened the door. He started to climb in and sit down when, suddenly, he let out a howl. Not a scared howl, but a pissed off howl. He started calling them everything in the book and by some names that weren't in the book, any book. He jumped down from his perch and threw an old, banged up, kid's booster seat across the main floor where it bounced off the side of the ladder truck. As the engine drove out the door, he was shaking his fist out the window and screaming in rage, "Fuckin' assholes! I'll get you! Fuckin' assholes!"

Is it possible to laugh any harder than those laddermen? Nah.

PIPES

The older guy on the group sidled up to the recently transferred-in younger guy and said, "C'mere for a minute. I want to show you something."

The younger guy followed along to the patrol desk.

The older guy pointed to the clock and said, "It's almost midnight. Every night at the same time, you have to do something."

"Okay," came the reply.

"When the midnight beep goes off, you have to turn the thermostat all the way."

"Okay," came the reply again.

"Want to know why?"

"Sure, I guess. Yeah."

"Okay then. Every night, the Captain watches the news until 11:30 and then goes to bed. By midnight, if we haven't had a run, he's just about all the way asleep. About 12:15 or so, the pipes will start banging like a son of a bitch. One of the biggest pipes is in the Captain's room, right next to his bed. The noise wakes him up and pisses him off, big time."

"You're kidding, right?"

"Nope."

Just then, the fire radio beeped.

It was midnight.

The older guy walked over to a corner of the main

floor and cranked the thermostat way up.

The younger fireman was laughing like hell.

Within fifteen minutes, the pipes were banging.

Within another five minutes, you could hear the Captain from his room, a floor above and in the front part of the firehouse, cursing and swearing at the top of his lungs.

The older guy walked over to the thermostat and turned it back down. Then he sat on the chair in the patrol desk and smiled a smile of complete satisfaction.

"Gets him every time," he concluded.

The Secret Amphibian

One fine day, as one of Boston's firemen was getting ready to leave home to work the night tour, one of his daughters appeared in the kitchen with a captured amphibian: a huge, gigantic frog. Unable to keep the amphibian in the house, the daughter was prepared to bring it back to a nearby body of water - where she's captured same - and release it. Her Dad had other ideas.

"Don't worry, honey," he offered as he looked around for a box. Finding one suitable for the task, he added "I'll do that for you. Here, put the frog in the box."

The fireman already had a mark in mind. When he

arrived at the fire house, he snuck upstairs and put the box on the floor inside the Captain's locker. Satisfied, all he had to do was wait.

The first payoff came early in the evening, about 6:30.

The guys were sitting in the kitchen having coffee and waiting for the next run. They'd already been out a half-dozen times and there seemed little use in climbing the stairs only to have to slide the pole again. It was always like this during busy tours and what it lacked in production - lots of false alarms - it made up for in bonding.

"Damndest thing I've ever heard," the Captain said.

"What's that Cap?" one man asked.

"Any of you guys hear frogs?"

Now, no one else knew anything about the prank and while they looked at the skipper quizzically, the prankster just about bit his lip off. He couldn't believe his good fortune! At best, he'd hoped for a nocturnal interruption but this . . . this . . . this was gold!

So he joined in.

"Frogs, Cap?"

"Yes, I swear I hear a frog croaking."

"Where?"

"I was in my office when I hear this croak. I thought I was hearing things. Then I heard it again. It was a frog. I'm sure of it. I stuck my head out the window and listened. Nothing."

The bells started to ring again. Up they jumped and out the door they flew.

They would repeat this many more times this night.

10 runs.

15 runs.

False alarms.

Rubbish fires.

Two tough building fires.

20 runs.

Then, finally, at 5:00 in the morning, coming back from the 23rd run of the tour, everyone was pooped. They'd consumed several gallons of half-way decent firehouse coffee and scoured the refrigerator for anything anyone may have left behind - or unattended. With the sun breaking over the horizon, everyone, save the man on watch, climbed the stairs looking for a place to crash. A bunk, a couch, there was even one asleep, stretched out on one of the kitchen benches.

It had been a typical summer night in a very busy District 7.

Even the Captain, a man of perpetual motion, had had enough for one night. He laid down on his bunk. On the edge, drifting off to nap land, he heard it again: *Ribbit . . . Ribbit.*

It was the frog again!

"What the . . . " the Captain said aloud as he sat up.

He sat and listened.

There is was again!

Ribbit . . . Ribbit.

The Captain stood up and walked toward where the sound seemed to be coming from.

Ribbit . . . Ribbit.

He stepped toward his locker.

Ribbit . . . Ribbit.

Louder!

He opened the door.

RIBBIT . . . RIBBIT.

The Captain stuck his foot behind the shoebox and kicked it out of his locker.

Louder yet!

RIBBIT . . . RIBBIT.

He reached down and carefully removed the top.

Out jumped a huge, gigantic frog!

So at sometime after 0515 on an otherwise promising morning, the firehouse was filled with a very loud and, it says here, a very well deserved admonition:

"Felson, you asshole!"

Alarm Clock

Same prankster.

Same Captain.

The former found an old alarm clock at home. The kind that doesn't make a ticking sound but has two very large alarm bells attached to the top.

The latter never knew the former had snuck into his office and tied said alarm clock to the spring under the mattress on his bunk.

Well, he never knew until 0430 when all of a sudden:

Ding! Ding! Ding! Ding! Ding!

GARTERS

That would be garter snakes, not garter belts. As in bring an elongated, legless reptile into the fire house and slide him (her?) under the blanket of the bunk upon which you know a snake-hating Vietnam veteran will lay on later with the hope of catching a few winks.

Then all you have to do is wait.

When your prank pays off – and it did – big time – you can rest assured that they'll never know it was you . . . can you dust a snake for fingerprints? Didn't think so.

RUBIK'S CUBE SOLVED!

We probably all remember the first time we saw a Rubik's Cube, or at least the first time we sat down and tried to solve the infernal puzzle. Years later we'd all marvel at the kids who could solve it in 30 seconds or less - because we'd spent hours and hours on the

BUSY AS HELL

damned thing and never even got one side all the same color, that's why.

But there was one guy who did it, a Lieutenant from a pretty busy engine company - one in the same fire house with the Division Commander. (Okay, the LT was on Engine 42.) The plan to deceive was hatched in pretty short order. Let's have some fun, he said to himself.

Much earlier, on the night in question, the aforementioned Division Commander - as terrific a guy as ever pulled on a pair of fire boots - found Rubik's Cube on the kitchen table. He asked someone what it was and when told, decided he'd have a go at solving the puzzle. So, he sat in his office, twisting and turning, looking and studying, twisting some more, cussing a bit, putting it down, picking it up again, twisting, turning, turning, twisting . . . until, finally, near midnight, the boss - who, remarkably, was still in his civilian clothes, such was Rubik's ability to transfix - had had enough. He walked into the kitchen and finding the Lieutenant and one or two firemen placed the cube on the table. "I give up," he said, almost sadly. "Maybe one of you guys can figure it out." Everyone shook their heads. No one wanted to pick up the gauntlet. Nope. Ain't happenin'.

Then later on, after returning from a run at about 3:00 AM, the Lieutenant wandered into the kitchen again and found himself alone with Rubik's wretched mystery.

So he decided to have a go at it.

He took it into his room.

And he solved it.

In about 30 minutes.

Then he quietly walked back into the kitchen and placed the cube on the kitchen table. All six sides were as they're supposed to be. One side white, one side yellow, one side red, one side blue, one side green, and one side orange.

So he waited.

His reward came at just before 7:00 AM when he went back into the kitchen for a cup of coffee and found the Division Commander sitting alone, holding the cube in his hand.

"You see this?" he asked the Lieutenant. "Goddamdest thing I've ever seen. I fooled around with this for hours and couldn't get one side the same color. Now look at it. I'm feeling pretty stupid right about now."

By now, the remaining members of the night crew had drifted into the kitchen.

They took turns being shocked.

Then they started looking around at each other.

"Did you do this?" they asked one another.

Everyone shook their heads in the negative.

Finally, the Division Commander noticed that there

was only one guy sitting at the table who didn't join the conversation.

He slowly turned to the Lieutenant, a broad smile breaking across his face and asked, "Mike, did you do this?"

"I cannot lie, Chief," I replied to John Harrison. "Yes, I did."

"How in the hell did you do it?"

"Just lucky, I guess."

Now, thirty something years later, I will come clean.

Did you readers know that the Rubik's Cube came apart?

That you could pry it open, unscrew it, fix the sides the right way and then put it all back together?

In about ten minutes?

Well, you can.

Trust me.

TELEPHONES

Back in the day - and isn't that a cute little phrase - the inter-firehouse telephone system was more primitive than it was destined to become as technology, such as it was, advanced. Where once you had to connect through the fire alarm office in order to reach another fire house, it was now possible to pick up the phone and dial the three-digit number of the company you wanted to reach. All such numbers started with 4. The second two numbers were always the number of the engine company occupying the fire house even if they were quartered with a ladder company. So, for instance, if you wanted to reach Engine 41, you dialed 441. If you wanted to reach Ladder 14 - in the same house with Engine 41 - you dialed the same 441.

This semi-modernization of the communication system became the storage locker for creative pranksters. There was no shortage of ammunition one could fire at gullible targets. All you had to do was call a fire house, make believe you were calling from fire alarm or some other official place, tell them to do something and unless they smelled a rat, they'd comply.

Probably the most common prank was to call a firehouse where you knew a new guy was on house watch - pranksters often worked with inside information - and dispatch them to a building fire, a building that just happened to be their very own fire house. Invariably, the new guy would answer the phone, take the information and hurriedly hit the house gong, turn on the house lights and loudly announce the location of the "burning building."

More than a few were victimized by this prank. And some of them, yes, more than once.

One such prankster - probably the King of Pranksters - once picked up the telephone and made the following call:

At about 10:00 PM, he dialed 407.

The phone was answered immediately.

"Fire fighter Jones, Engine 7."

"Yeah, this is the motor squad. Have Ladder 17 report to the shop right away. We need to change the piece immediately."

"Ah, okay."

Trap set, hook swallowed.

The man of watch called the officer of Ladder 17 on the intercom and told him about the phone call. One can imagine the reaction:

"Ay, Loo, the shop just called. They want you down to change the piece. They said immediately. Sounds serious."

"What? Change the truck? What the hell is wrong with these people?! Why can't they do this crap in the daytime?"

"Want me to have the guys come down?"

"Yeah, please."

The man on watch hits the button on the PA system and says, "Ladder 17 to the main floor. You're going to the shop."

So down the stairs they came, grumbling all the way.

Ladder 17's fire fighters climbed aboard their ladder truck and off they went.

But you already know what happened, don't you.

Ladder 17 arrived at the shop. The Lieutenant went inside to inquire about the pending change of apparatus. The man in the shop told them he had no idea what he was talking about. The King of Pranksters strikes again!

Another of his more famous pranks was to inquire about the presence of certain chief officers.

He'd call a company, especially at night and ask, simply, "Did the deputy get there yet?"

"Ah . . . ah . . . the deputy? No."

"Okay. When he does, have him call fire alarm, okay?"

"Ah, yeah. Sure."

Of course the man who answered would race to the officer and sound the alarm: "Loo, the deputy's on his way!"

"The deputy? What the hell does he want?"

"No clue but fire alarm called and asked if he was here yet. I told them he wasn't. They said that when he gets here we should have him call them."

Another trap set, another hook swallowed.

Of course the King of Pranks just sat back in his chair, closed his eyes and smiled a contented smile . . . wondering what manner of panic he had set in motion with a simple phone call to an unsuspecting chump.

Then one night it happened. The prankster was done in by a prank and to make matters even more delicious, it was a prank of his own doing! And to put the cherry on top, he didn't even know it was a prank for at least fifteen minutes.

Here's the scene:

It's about quarter to 11:00. The King of Pranks was on house watch when the phone rang. Dutifully, he answered with his name and company. He listened carefully as the man on the other end of the call told him to take Engine 10 to a general alarm fire in Swampscott, a seaside town about thirteen miles north of Boston. He acknowledged the order, put the phone down and thought to himself, I'm not falling for that! Who the hell do these people think they're playing with?

So he went back to watching TV and waiting for the bells to ring. Some things never change.

Then, at precisely 11:00 PM, the news came on. Guess what the top news story was? You guessed it, the general alarm fire in Swampscott. The same big fire the fire alarm office had told him to have his company respond to!

No one can be sure what was running though his mind but I'm sure it wasn't a pleasant time. For starters, he had to go upstairs to the officer's room and confess. Immediately! They were supposed to be at a fire a dozen miles away but instead here they sat, in the fire house.

"Ah, Loo," he said, "I screwed up. Big."

Fortunately, the boss didn't panic. We all know some officers who would have launched themselves through the roof, right? Not this guy. Instead, he slid the pole, went outside to the pay phone and called fire alarm. When they answered, he asked to speak to Engine 10, his own company. The man in fire alarm told him that Engine 10 wasn't available because - yup - they were at a big fire in Swampscott. The Lieutenant came back inside, summoned his crew to the main floor, opened the overhead door and off they went - no sirens, no red lights, just another vehicle on the road to Swampscott.

A New Kind Of Fire Engine

Legend has it that a singular duo - and were they ever singular - took it upon themselves to devise a new system for responses by fire engines in areas of the city where traffic was always a problem. The fact that they were (and presumably, remain) certifiable nut jobs will add some spice to the story.

Our case in point is the fire house situated at 941 Boylston Street - home to Engine 33 and Ladder 15 - a main thoroughfare that connects downtown Boston to an area called The Fenway. Yes, that Fenway. Where the Red Sox play.

Boylston Street is a very busy and congested retail area, boasting top-end retail stores, restaurants, hotels, and a myriad of other commercial entities. (In 2013, it was the scene of what became known as the Marathon Bombing.) On any average day, there is no shortage of traffic and pedestrians and, so, commotion.

The fire house is equipped with an extra tool or two to help the companies maneuver through the chaos when they have a run - there's a switch that turns the lights red and another that sets off an outside siren. When both are activated, the traffic stops and the people do, too. Everyone is watching the fire house, waiting for the fire engines to respond. For the drivers, I suppose it's a nuisance. But the pedestrians always seemed to think it was pretty cool. Many took pictures of events as they unfolded.

Then, one day, the singular duo decided to display their new kind of fire engine for all to see.

One of them hit the switch to set of the siren, hit the other switch to turn the traffic lights red and then a third switch to raise the overhead doors.

The stage was set.

The audience waited with bated breath

Then, right on cue, the second part of the duo, dressed in his rubber coat and helmet, drove out the front door... on a bicycle! With an axe on his shoulder, he turned left and headed down Boylston Street.

Listening In

Someone brought one of those special, repairman telephones into the firehouse - the kind used by the phone company people to check phone lines. At first it didn't seem like such a big deal. Until . . . until we learned that if you connected the two alligator clips to a small connection box in the patrol desk, you could listen to the people talking on the pay phone outside. And even better, you could actually flip a little switch and, get this, talk to them!

We had a guy in there one night - oh my God, it was hilarious - and one of us kept flipping the switch and saying "Please deposit five cents for another minute," and then switching it off before the poor guy had a chance to reply. He must have put a dollars worth of nickels in that phone and never got to complete his call.

We could hear him yelling into the phone, "Operator! OPERATOR!"

Click.

"Please deposit another five cents."

Click.

"OPERATOR! Goddammit answer me!"

Click.

"Please deposit another five cents."

Click.

This went on for twenty minutes, at least.

The good news? Well, because the call was never even dialed, much less completed, when he pushed the coin return lever down, all his nickels came back. He tried his call again and of course, this time we left him alone.

Fire Muses Are Real. No, Really.

The engine company and its crew of four rolled up to the big overhead door at the car wash on Columbia Road. The ladder company, equally manned, was right behind. There was a smoke oozing out from the edges of the door. Through the window, you could see a small fire on the floor. The smell was unmistakable. It was a rubbish fire. No big deal. Run a line, squirt some water, and get the hell out of there.

But the Fire Muses had other ideas. Now, if you don't believe in Fire Muses then, well, you don't believe that there is song and dance and poetry to be found in the movements of firemen as they handle their tasks. But, we'll get to that in just a minute.

One the laddermen forced the small office-type door open and once inside located the button for the overhead door. He pressed the button and the door opened wide.

The engine guys started an inch-and-a-half line inside and stood by as the pipe man pulled the nozzle handle back a bit and started operating on the small fire. Piece of cake, right?

Then the same ladderman found a series of switches

and decided to help by turning the lights on. Smart move. Usually.

Enter the Fire Muses.

Suddenly, the car wash revved up and started operating!

Lights flashed as the machinery roared to life.

Giant brushes started spinning and bouncing up and down!

Now back in those days, we wore nifty little gadgets called wheat lights. They consisted of a small lamp attached to a long, thick electrical cord that was, in turn, attached to a large wet-cell battery. The battery had loops on the back so that the entire gadget could be worn around the waist on a leather belt.

Well, that wire proved to be a problem courtesy of the Fire Muses who, about this time, decided to prove that poetry of movement exists in a car wash on fire. They reached out with their invisible hands and attached the electric cord on the pipe man's wheat light to one of the brushes and decided to take him for a ride.

Up and down he went, back and forth.

Push back, pull up.

Round and round.

Like a rag doll.

Water was going every-damned-where because he hung onto the line like the professional he was while the

Fire Muses had their fun with him.

Did anyone help him?

Nope. Not immediately.

We were too busy laughing like hell. The kind of laughter that makes you bend over and grab your stomach, those old fashioned belly laughs that bring tears to your eyes.

And I still don't remember how he got loose - or when.

Rivalries

Inter-company rivalries took many forms. While the rivalries were all in fun, there were a few times when the stakes were a tad higher. Would you believe that one Lieutenant was well known for arriving at a location, finding a building on fire, and waiting until his pump was set up his line run before he got on the radio and asked for more help? Of course, he didn't do this very often but let's just say he did it more than once. In every instance, the fire was in a well-known vacant building where we'd had a few fires before - we used to call such buildings "drill towers." It seems outrageous but that's what it was like back then. There were so many fires in so many vacant buildings. They (kids?) would light them on fire just for the hell of it, as many times as they could before the city finally got around to tearing them down.

Some of the friendly rivalries became a game of geography, one you willingly played and one you wanted to win.

For example, being listed as the first due company and being beaten to the location by the second due company was a mortal sin. It was inexcusable! There was pride in being where you were supposed to be, when you were supposed to be there. If there was a fire, making sure you beat the next closest engine company in the front door with a line was your mission. (NOTE: Every fireman knows what "first due" means. Or at least they should. The first due engine and truck are the two closest companies to a location, usually a box location at an intersection. The designation is based on geography. The second and third due are, naturally, second and third closest to the location. Over the years, the designation first due has been hijacked and so, to some, it means the first company to arrive. It doesn't. No matter who arrives first, the first due company never changes. It's always the closest company. Do companies arrive out of order? Of course. But it doesn't change who's first due.)

We were always reminded that it was impossible to make up lost time on the road by driving too fast. Instead, we were trained to get on the fire engine and out of the fire house as quickly as possible. It may seem almost unbelievable these days but during the war years it was very common for a company to clear the floor in 30-seconds or less. That's right, 30-seconds or less, i. e., from the time the house gong went off until the front bumper went over the threshold. The house gong was the ultimate summons.

For a competitive company filled with hard-charging officers and equally hard-charging firemen, learning that an officer in a neighboring engine company took his sweet-ass time responding was a bonanza. At first we didn't believe the rumors.

However, the inter-departmental grapevine - i.e., complaints from his crew - verified the truth: this particular guy, while a smart, competent officer, felt put upon because he had to respond to so many false alarms. So he stopped sliding the pole to reach the apparatus floor; he took the stairs instead. He decided to punish those who pulled false alarms by, again, taking his sweet-ass time getting out the door.

We still hustled out the door on every run and, so, regularly arrived at his first due locations ahead of him and his crew - they hated it like sin but the officer didn't care. Granted, many of our runs were false alarms and the wisdom of flying out the door to what was almost assuredly another one was often challenged. But a valuable lesson had been learned many years earlier and passed down to us. Our company had gone to a false alarm at the same nearby location eight times between 6:00 pm and midnight....and then, at 3:00 AM, they responded to the same location.

Another false alarm?

Nope.

Two-alarm fire on the same corner.

The lesson was (and remains) clear. Our job was to be there when we were called and the sooner the better.

Also, there was no small measure of bravado attached to being the busiest company, in a district, division or city-wide. The statistics might vary slightly from year to year but critical analysis reveals that some of the same fire companies were in the top five for 50 years running. For example, Ladders 4, 7, 12, 13, 23, and 30 seemed to occupy the top spots every year going all the way back to the 1930s. Today, it's interesting to note that three of those trucks (12, 13, 30) have been disbanded while the other three (4, 7, 23) are still among the top ten for runs and fire duty.

The spirit of competition wasn't embraced by everyone, though. I'm reminded of an early December evening when one of the busier trucks responded for the 5000th time that year. They arrived at the box location, determined it was a false alarm and headed back to the fire house with the message: "Box 3113 is false and now having responded for the five-thousandth time this year, we're returning."

Somewhere in the city, a wholly unimpressed though enterprising fireman raced to his fire engine, switched on the ignition, grabbed the transmitter, and offered this retort: "700 runs. Same money."

Ouch.

Tow Jack

If this was an episode of the The Twilight Zone, Rod Serling would undoubtedly introduce our next character like this:

"You're traveling through another dimension, a dimension not only of sight and sound but of mind; a journey into a wondrous land whose boundaries are that of imagination. Our case in point, one District Fire Chief, a man so thoroughly determined to eliminate illegal parking in his district that the local cops gave him a nickname, one not based on love and caring, but one of not-at-all-subtle derision - call it hatred - because he was a world class pain in the ass. They called him "Tow Jack."

At this point, the black and white image on your television screen would fade to a scene of a place called Tow Truck Heaven.

Heaven?

Yes. Because if driving a tow truck was your business, this particular fire chief made you a fortune. He could keep a fleet of hooks busy for hours. Oh brother, did Tow Jack drive them crazy!

You see, shortly after arriving at his new assignment

in District 3, he set out on a one-man crusade to remove every single illegally parked car, truck, van, bus, and RV from the area which includes all of Beacon Hill (and its narrow, quirky, cobblestone streets), Downtown Crossing, the streets surrounding the Mass. General Hospital, City Hall and the State House, the waterfront along Atlantic Avenue and Commercial Street, the North End, Faneuil Hall Market Place, and, well, just about any place where it is borderline impossible to find a parking place.

He was a man on a mission. He was relentless. He missed not a single illegally parked vehicle.

And he didn't give a hoot what anyone thought about him.

His goal was to keep the area clear for fire engines to operate, you know, just in case they had a fire? A possibility that the average double-parker never thinks about when he or, yes, she blocks traffic or parks in front of a hydrant.

Yes, Tow Jack was a pain in the ass.

But he was right. 100 percent.

BUSY AS HELL

GET THE HELL OUT OF THE WAY!

The fire engine is responding to a fire some distance away. The Captain tells the pump operator to go down Columbia Road and jump on I-93 North - the highway that slices through Boston - and head for downtown.

So far, so good.

Sirens wailing, air horns blasting, the company makes decent time.

Until they hit the onramp to I-93.

Gridlock.

Cars and trucks are scrambling to get out of the way but there really isn't anywhere to go.

It's a mess.

Growing impatient, the captain decides to take action. He picks up the handset for the loud speaker mounted on the roof and starts ordering the cars to move.

"This is the Boston Fire Department responding to a fire! Move all the way to the right!"

Yes, motorists are trying to get out of the way of the siren and air horn but nothing much changes.

The captain mutters to himself, "Goddammit. What the hell is wrong with these people?"

In his distinctive voice, he tries again.

"Move all the way to the right! This is an emergency vehicle responding to a fire! Move all the way to the right!"

Still no real change.

"Get out of the way! Move over!"

The captain is furious. He throws the loud speaker handset against the windshield.

"Goddammit!" he yells.

Finally, the driver, amused, yells over, "Hey Cap, why don't you say that over the loudspeaker instead of the fire department radio."

Like Father, Like Son

The famous and oft-recorded Steve Goodman song, City of New Orleans, contains the words:

The sons of Pullman porters and the sons of engineers, ride their father's magic carpets made of steel.

The suggestion, of course, is that riding trains for a living is a family affair, a career passed along from great grandfathers to grandfathers to fathers to sons to sons to sons. Well, so too was the BFD although, unlike their rail-riding counterparts, our forefathers chose to ride hand-me-down magic carpets shaped like big red fire engines. I'd expect a debate from the rail-rider families about which was more fun to do.

But I do know that since at least the late 1800s, over hundreds of thousands of dinners at thousands of Boston dinner tables, stories, tall tales, legends and yarns about the city and its firemen have found their way to family trees; the branches of some having been filled with the names of those who picked up the family gauntlet, waited for the bells to ring and then jumped aboard the red fire engines hell bent for who knows where.

But what makes someone want to run into burning buildings while all the sane people are running out? What's the attraction? Good question - one I've asked myself for fifty years.

Perhaps New York City Chief Edward F. Coker said it best in 1910:

"I have no ambition in this world but one, and that is to be a firefighter The position may, in the eyes of some, appear to be a lowly one; but we who know the work which the firefighter has to do believe that his is a noble calling. There is an adage, which says that 'Nothing can be destroyed except by fire.' We strive to preserve from destruction the wealth of the world which is the product of the industry of men, necessary for the comfort of both the rich and the poor. We are defenders from fires of the art, which has beautified the world, the product of the genius of men and the means of refinement of mankind. (But, above all; our proudest endeavor is to save lives of men-the work of God Himself. Under the impulse of such thoughts, the nobility of the occupation thrills us and stimulates us to deeds of daring, even at the supreme sacrifice. Such considerations may not strike the average mind, but they are sufficient to fill to the limit our ambition in life and to make us serve the general purpose of human society."

At first glance, the temptation might be to accept that the simple axiom "helping people" is a driving force behind someone's interest in joining the fire service. Count me among those who will reject this notion because you can never know what awaits you at the end of the run. There is no guarantee that there's a person in trouble or distress awaiting the arrival of the fire engines.

On the other hand, for example, take nurses - they always help people. That's because they help patients and patients are people. Nurses don't generally wait for a bell to ring before they race off somewhere to see a patient either. In fact, most of the time, their patients come to them. So, while nurses become nurses to "help people," firemen probably don't.

Of course, it's entirely possible that more mainstream concerns - issues like job security, health insurance, salaries, etc. - enter someone's career-minded thought process but when lumped together as a group, they are unlikely to outweigh the sheer excitement of just being a fireman.

Those who choose the family path are infected with a palpable dose of an interest in satisfying oneself and ones perception of what makes life exciting. The first attraction might be the noise: the gong clangs and siren howls. Add red lights, urgency, speed, commotion and a borderline unhealthy adrenaline spike to the formula and it's easy to see the attraction; racing out of the fire house and careening through the streets at full throttle is a rush. I trust that the most stone-faced Las Vegas card dealers would be similarly affected.

What of the job itself?

What of racing in when everyone else is racing out?

What of the lives inside - those in need of saving?

The fire advances and puts people and property in jeopardy. It's the fireman's job to put as much water as possible - as quickly as possible - on the barraging enemy and between anything needing saving.

What makes someone, anyone, want to do any of this?

Now, while I cannot speak for others, I believe I know the answer.

It's the gauntlet.

It's the battle, the fight.

It's the combat, the Us vs. Them.

It's the same rush that makes Marines and soldiers and sailors and airmen charge toward the sound of the guns. There's a certain something inside a fireman that clicks when a mortal enemy stands in your face and dares you to engage.

This father to son thing - it's an affliction as old as time.

It's tough work; it's dangerous work.

But it's a helluva lot of fun, too.

Good Jakes Everywhere

Jakes.

That's what Boston firemen call their counterparts.

The term can supposedly be traced back to pre-radio days when firemen carried a J-shaped key and used it to unlock fire boxes so they could send messages in Morse Code to the fire alarm office. J Key was shortened to jakey and finally to jake. At least that's the rumor.

As the term gained acceptance, firemen became known as good jakes and great jakes, subjective terms that beg discussion and interpretation. At the core of the issue is the desire of some to crown certain firemen as "the best jake" without offering any means of authentication save an ability to mix a playful personality with mainstream fire ground abilities. For the record, some who were deemed to be the "best fireman ever" weren't even the best firemen on their own company, let alone in the history of the BFD. It's interesting to note that quite often, these lofty evaluations have been made by members who never worked with the fireman in question or, worse, by people altogether outside the department.

So then, let's get this over with:

There is no such thing as "the best jake."

During the war years, Boston's fire companies were filled with good jakes and great jakes.

Being on a busy company didn't mean you were better than someone on a slow company.

Going to more fires didn't mean you were better, either.

There were more than enough fires to go around, and if you weren't a decent jake, you didn't last very long.

So then, for the purposes of this book, I have chosen to write about two great jakes who were well know to many during the war years. I'm sure there were dozens of firemen who were just as good at what they did, but, well, these two guys lost the coin toss and will have their greatness cut in half, sliced, diced, and analyzed:

BIG JOHN

One man who stood out among his peers is also one of Boston's legendary firemen, John Gaddis. Big John spent the bulk of his stellar thirty-four-year career riding on Ladder 4, as tough an assignment as there was. Going back as far as the 1920s, Ladder 4 has consistently been in the top five ladder trucks for runs and workers. It is the most often decorated company in BFD history - John owns two pieces of that history. He received the John E. Fitzgerald Medal for the Most Meritorious Act (1962) and the Walter Scott Medal for Valor (1967), the latter awarded for a "display of exceptional valor." The incident occurred during the riots of June 1967 when, as Ladder 4 was preparing to return to quarters, a sniper opened fire on them - one jake reported hearing ten rounds being fired - and Fire Lieutenant Joe Donovan fell to the ground, wounded. Big John immediately went to the aid of Lieutenant Donovan and dragged him around the front of the truck to the opposite side.

Like so many of his WWII comrades in arms, John was a study in stoicism. He never said much and when he did talk, it wasn't for very long. If you looked up Strong Silent Type in your Webster's unabridged, you'd see John's picture. He was also a terrific roof man, the kind of guy who had chopped holes in any number of different type roofs along the way - enough chopping to reach all the way to China especially if you kept your axe sharp and ready to go - which the old-timers always did. Personally, I didn't have to chop many holes in roofs in my years. This is true because (thankfully) there always seemed to be someone a lot more interested in climbing on smokey, slippery, dangerous rooftops than I.

One snowy afternoon comes to mind because I got to see something I'd never seen before and never saw again. While we pushed a line into an attic on Sargent Street, the kind with no ventilation except one tiny window at the other end of the building, the Lieutenant leaned over and spoke in my ear. "We'll be okay in a minute. The roof man is here," he said quietly. Admittedly, I was puzzled. I mean how does the pipe man on an engine company deployed on a narrow attic stairway get to watch a roof man in action?

Easy.

Watch John Gaddis.

You see, Ladder 4 couldn't get close enough to the building to throw their aerial ladder and there wasn't enough time (or manpower) to drag a fifty foot ground ladder from the truck, lug it through the snow and get it to the roof. So, what does the Big John do?

Again, easy.

He walked into the building, found the charged line of hose and followed it up the stairs. Then he found the pipe man and the officer trying to make the last couple of stairs. He leaned over to the boss and asked if he could get up there beside them. The boss smiled and nodded. John crawled up the last couple of steps and came into the attic with us. Then, get this, he stood up straight and with a rake, not an axe, punched a big hole in the roof. In an instant....smoke gone, heat gone. Piece of cake.

Mr. Rogers

His Christian name is Kenneth Joseph Rogers. As expected, we called him Kenny. Yet, through the years he acquired a very official sounding, old English-type, upscale title . . . Mister. As in Mr. Rogers. Hey, even chiefs called him Mr. Rogers.

Now some would suggest the obvious - that the title was a spin-off from the PBS television show, *Mr. Roger's Neighborhood*. It wasn't. Even Kenny doesn't know for sure where the title came from, although he suspects his old friend Jimmy Freeman was responsible.

If there is one constant in Kenny's life, it's the Boston Fire Department. I'd challenge anyone - and I do mean anyone - to come forward with the name of a man more devoted or more dedicated to the job. Of the 39 years, 6 months, and 13 days Kenny served the citizens of Boston, he gave his all during every tour of duty. He dove in head first. He never came up for air and never, ever took a single step backwards. You see, Kenny's approach was simple....

He believed that "working" meant doing everything possible during every single hour of every single tour of duty to make the job better for us - the firemen - and, so, for the people we were sworn to protect. He believed that we provided a much needed service to the people outside the fire house doors and, dammit, that, no matter what, we should be there when they called us.

Kenny believed in adding red lights to the fire engine, not because he was some weirdo light freak, but because they made responding firemen more visible and, therefore, safer.

He believed in adding extra Scotchlite™ company numbers to the fire engine so company members could see it and find it from everywhere.

Kenny criticized the city administration when they reduced the initial response to a pulled box by 60% in certain parts of Boston - where two-thirds of the fires were - while continuing to send a three engine, two truck response to areas where about one-third of the fires happen.

He criticized them when they claimed the reduced assignments were a tool to curb false alarm responses because, in the process, the policy proved they had more concern for the life hazard in one-third of the city than they did in the other two-thirds.

Kenny kept a police scanner operating in the fire house because cops ride around all day and night when they're on patrol. They often find fires before the civilian population does. When they do, they tell their dispatcher over the radio and thus alert firemen who have police scanners operating. So, if the fire is nearby, company members will know about the fire even before our own fire alarm office does.

He played Christmas music over the PA system in the fire engine and later from the chief's car. People waved and smiled. Kenny waved and smiled right back. It was great PR.

Kenny believed there was a right way and a wrong way to do things. It wasn't just his opinion; it was the common sense approach to all things fire department. He took it upon himself to help teach every new fireman who showed up in the fire house how to do things the right way.

The one thing we all appreciated most about Kenny was his technical proficiency. He always knew what he was doing and just didn't make mistakes. He excelled at everything. When pushing a line inside, he never hesitated or, again, never took a single step backwards. When he drove the pump, he always knew where he was going, and if we had a fire, the joke used to be that we didn't need a hydrant because Kenny could get water out of a mailbox.

Kenny is the quintessential raconteur, a wonderfully animated spinner of yarns complete with dead-on accurate sound effects. But his humor wasn't confined to stories in the kitchen....consider the message he delivered to a brand new guy who, after accidentally gulping a belly full of smoke, panicked, and then ran outside. As the lad raced down the stairs, Kenny yelled after him, "Hey, kid, if you're gonna puke, hide your helmet so nobody knows you're from Engine 24!"

If Bostonians had to choose one player from National Hockey League history to start a new league from scratch, they would (and properly) choose Bobby Orr.

Well, if I had to choose one fireman from the Boston Fire Department's history to start a new fire department from scratch, I'd choose Kenny Rogers.

It was an honor and privilege to work with him.

Line Of Duty Deaths

The following named members of the Boston Fire Department were killed in the line of duty during the years 1963-1983. In all, thirty-eight members lost their lives protecting the people of Boston - that's roughly one every 6 ½ months.

October 1, 1964

Lieutenant John J. McCorkle, Engine 24
Lieutenant John J. Geswell, Ladder 26
Fire Fighter Robert J. Clougherty, Engine 3
Fire Fighter Francis L. Murphy, Engine 24
Fire Fighter James B. Sheedy, Ladder 4

All five men were killed when a wall of a vacant 4-story factory, located at 34 Trumbull Street, collapsed and buried them. This has forever been known as the "Trumbull Street Fire."

January 7, 1967

Chief of Department James J. Flanagan

Killed by motorist when he stopped to assist a motorist who had been involved in an accident on the South East Expressway.

November 23, 1967

Lieutenant Warren T. Lynch, Engine Squad 18
Died from smoke inhalation while working in the attic of a house at 49 Hartford Street, Roxbury.

November 23, 1968

District Chief Richard Sullivan Jr., District 2
Collapsed and died while assisting on-duty members at a fire in Hyde Park.

March 3, 1970

Lieutenant George J. Gottwald, Rescue Pumper
Died of injuries he received while battling a fire at 2235 Washington Street, Roxbury.

October 16, 1970

Lieutenant Joseph J. Downing, Engine 2
Died from injuries and severe burns after a taxicab's gasoline tank exploded in front of 18 Dorchester Street, South Boston and engulfed him in fire.

BUSY AS HELL

December 30, 1970

Fire Fighter Edwin H. Foley, Engine 30
Killed when he fell from the fire engine and was run over. He was responding to a false alarm.

July 4, 1971

Fire Fighter Jeremiah Collins, Engine 45
Killed when a building in the Mt. Calvary Cemetery partially collapsed on him.

August 17, 1971

Lieutenant Daniel T. McInness, Engine 8
Died of a heart attack after responding to an alarm in the Charlestown Navy Yard.

November 5, 1971

Fire Fighter James F. Doneghy, Ladder 30
Killed when thrown from the tiller seat of the apparatus while responding to Box 2388.

Mike Foley

November 22, 1971

Fire Fighter Patrick J. Kelly, Engine 26
Killed when he fell five floors down an elevator shaft at 132-144 Lincoln Street, Downtown.

May 11, 1972

Fire Fighter John A. Hopkins, Engine 34
Killed after being crushed between the ladder truck and the firehouse doorframe while responding to Box 51.

June 17, 1972

Fire Fighter Richard B. Magee, Engine 33
Lieutenant Thomas J. Carroll, Engine 32
Fire Fighter Paul J. Murphy, Engine 32
Fire Fighter Thomas W. Beckwith, Engine 32
Fire Fighter Joseph F. Boucher, Engine 22
Fire Fighter John E. Jameson, Engine 22
Lieutenant John E. Hanbury, Ladder 13
Fire Fighter Charles E. Dolan, Ladder 13
Fire Fighter Joseph P. Saniuk, Ladder 13

All nine men were killed when the rear portion of the Hotel Vendome collapsed and buried them under four floors of debris.

BUSY AS HELL

June 19, 1972

Fire Fighter Vincent Dimino, Ladder 30
Killed when he was thrown from the tiller seat of Ladder 30 while responding to Box 2394.

February 2, 1973

Fire Fighter Arthur L. Ceurvels, Ladder 20
Killed while responding to Box 7311. FF Ceurvels was crushed between the tractor and trailer of Ladder 20 when the truck jack-knifed during a severe ice storm.

October 14, 1973

Fire Fighter John W. Carlson, Engine 28
Collapsed and died of died of a heart attack after operating at a building fire, 28 Cranston Street, Jamaica Plain, Box 2416.

January 22, 1974

Fire Fighter Bernard G. Tully, Engine 30
Died of injuries he received when Engine 30 collided with a garbage truck on a very icy morning while responding to a Still Alarm.

Mike Foley

March 6, 1974

Lieutenant James Flahive, Rescue 1

On October 22, 1946, Lieutenant James Flahive was severely injured when he inhaled smoke and poison gases from burning fur in the basement of Kakas Furs, 70-72 Chauncy Street, Downtown. Lieutenant Flahive died 27 years and 4 months later, never having regained consciousness. He was 67.

June 4, 1975

Lieutenant Hubert F. Moran, Ladder 6

Killed while fighting a fire in a vacant house at 38 Jones Avenue, Box 3535.

October 23, 1976

Fire Fighter Richard P. Sheridan, Ladder 16

Killed when a wall collapsed at a vacant factory at 22 Simmons Street, Roxbury, 3 alarms Box 2241.

April 11, 1977

Fire Fighter Hugh F. O'Brien, Ladder 5

Died from injuries sustained while fighting a brush fire near Bellevue Hill.

BUSY AS HELL

February 7, 1978

Fire Fighter John Joseph McDonough, LP 1
Died of a heart attack while responding to Box 1412 during the "Blizzard of '78."

November 27, 1978

Fire Fighter Robert M. Greene, Ladder 23
Died of multiple injuries suffered when he fell from a building on Alpha Road, Dorchester, Box 3323.

January 6, 1981

Lieutenant Paul M. Lentini, Engine 37
Fire Fighter James M. Gibbons, Engine 37
Fire Lieutenant Lentini and Fire Fighter Gibbons died while operating at a building fire at 16-17 Arlington Street, Back Bay, when part of the upper floors collapsed, trapping them and four other members for hours.

November 6, 1983

Fire Fighter Edward J. Donovan, Rescue 1
Died of injuries received after falling down a pole hole in quarters at 123 Oliver Street, Downtown.

MIKE FOLEY

ABOUT THE AUTHOR

Fire Lt. Mike Foley was a third generation Boston fire fighter who followed closely in the footsteps of his grandfather, District Chief "Iron Mike" Foley and his Dad, Lt. Bob Foley.

His website is BFDBusyAsHell.com

Read an excerpt from *Rescued Hearts*, a novel by Mike Foley.

RESCUED HEARTS

Grizzled Boston Fire Fighter veteran, Matt Toomey, has grown increasingly bitter and cynical as the decades have passed. His experiences in life have not only driven a wedge between him and the Catholic Church, but have also led him to turn his back on God altogether.

When his sister, a Catholic nun, becomes the victim of a violent crime, Matt initially finds his attitude toward life confirmed by the tragedy. But, in time, he discovers God is at work to lead him down a path to renewal.

CHAPTER 2
DORCHESTER, MASSACHUSETTS
NOVEMBER 29 - 7:50 PM

The fire house PA system crackled loudly, "Captain . . ." Matt sat bolt upright in his bunk. " . . . please come to the main floor."

As suddenly as they had besieged him, the little girl and the dream she haunts came crashing down in a blazing heap.

The youthful voice repeated, "Captain Toomey? Please come to the main floor."

Hands flat beside him and pressed into the old

mattress for support, Matt paused to catch his breath and get his bearings. He hadn't wanted to fall asleep. He just wanted to lay down and see if he could relieve some of the back pain he was feeling after what turned out to be a routine fire two hours ago. It would have been a lot worse if not for the young guys, he thought. They did all the bull work.

Mindful that he had been summoned, the middle-aged Fire Captain swung his tired legs over the side of the bunk and sat briefly, fearing that if he stood too fast, his legs would give out from under him. You would think that being startled awake would become old hat after 30-something years of working in the busiest fire houses in Boston, he reasoned. Yet, no matter how many thousands of times it had happened, there remained something uncivilized about being forcibly snatched away from a sound sleep and sent on a mission to God-knows-where.

Finally, satisfied his legs were still part of the rest of his body, Matt pushed his six-foot frame to a standing position with both hands. His mind was bounding forward at top speed: I never had a paunch in front before, what does being startled awake do to a 56-year old heart?, what day is it?, how long was I asleep?

The latter thought required but a quick glance at the clock on the wall opposite his bunk - it was just before eight o'clock - before, finally, "What's with this infernal dream!" he asked himself out loud.

Closing his eyes to gather his senses, Matt unconsciously fingered the small, gold crucifix hanging around his neck, the one he had worn every day for over forty years. It was an Easter gift from his mother and his wearing it represented the fulfillment of a pledge he made to her. "Promise me you'll keep it close to you and God will protect you," she had claimed. Certainly, Matt had survived some difficult times in thirty-three years of fighting fires and at times he wondered about its power. But he never knew, nor did anyone, whether his relative lack of serious injury had anything to do with God's protection because he wore a piece of man-made jewelry, or whether, like his cynical side believed, it was just coincidence. But one way or the other, Matt just ignored Godly details and accepted whatever life dished out. He believed in reality, not whether God really could affect things on Earth. Besides, and assuming God did protect him from harm, where was His willingness to protect him in other matters? he thought. Like protecting me from my own stupidity, protecting my children from my failures as a father, protecting little babies so they won't die in fires, what about them? There were no answers, of course, for this is where his one-sided, philosophical discussions with God always ended: with him asking why and God remaining silent.

Made in the USA
Charleston, SC
08 April 2016